# If you're not smiling, why not, because Seth is

*Seth showed an enlarged tummy and what we thought was a rash on his tor* *on Saturday 12th May, 2012. Sunday morning the "rash" had spread and his* *enlarged so we went to our Doctor. The Dr did a blood test and explained th* *enlarged due to him having an enlarged spleen and the rash was actually bru.....y. A rush is red, this was blue/purple and looked like he'd drawn dots with a pen all over his body. Something was wrong, his blood wasn't clotting. The Dr told us to stay home and stay isolated. That is how we spent Mothers Day 2012 until approximately 6pm that night when the phone rang. It was the Dr. She told me that she'd spoken to the E.D. Registrar at Monash Hospital in Clayton and she was waiting for Seth. I asked questions, lots of questions and kept getting told to get him to the E.D. urgently. Finally with a very calm voice, our Dr told me to hang up the phone and pack a bag for a stay in hospital, if I didn't, she would hang up and call an Ambulance. Every single possible part of my inner strength was used not to fall apart and just fall to the floor and cry. We didn't know what Seth had. Nikki and I already suspected Leukaemia earlier in the day and hoped we were wrong. Seth and Nikki drove to the E.D. Holly and I stayed home. I sat up all night, mobile phone on one leg and house phone on my other leg. Nikki was up all night in the E.D. whilst Seth had more tests and observations started. I finally decided to get Holly's bag ready for Child Care. At some point before Holly woke, Nikki called. The call I was waiting all night for, the call I hoped was to say Seth was on some medication and they were on their way home. It wasn't. Nikki called to tell me that Seth had Leukaemia. The Dr's didn't know what type and were going to do more tests, but he needed blood transfusions, lots. Then he'll start Chemotherapy.*

*Nikki was in the E.D. with Seth and my Mum. I needed to wake Holly I needed to hold her I needed to be with Seth. Holly was 13 months old, Seth was 5.*

*I took Holly to Child Care and tried to tell them where Seth was and why, in the end the carer worked out what I was trying to say and gave me her mobile phone number. She told me she will look after Holly and if I can't get back to her, she will take her home and give her dinner.*

*I got to the E.D. just as my mum was leaving to organise leave from her work and get some clothes etc that we might need. Not long later and Seth was wheeled down the corridor and into a place called the "Children's Cancer Centre" (CCC) with Nikki and I beside him. The information had already started forms that needed signatures had already been signed and it all seemed so numb. Later that day Seth was admitted into a single room up in the Children's Ward, he came home 13 days later with T-Cell Acute Lymphoblastic Leukaemia.*

*Nikki and I alternated between staying in hospital and home, spending time with Holly. The home phone had messages on it from friends and strangers every day. I returned every single call, whether I knew the person or not and subsequently developed a fear for the phone because it was the same bad news for every call. I developed an email contact list that I called "Catching up with Seth" that I sent out when new information was given to us.*

*Here are those emails; some information is incorrect, although at the time of writing them, I thought the information was correct.*

## Chapter 1

# 2012

**15/05/12**

Hi,

This week the most wonderful and fantastic five year old boy I have ever met, Seth has been diagnosed with Acute Lymphoblastic Leukaemia. He is in high spirits and will be in hospital until mid next week.

He will be having an intense 28 days with treatment and once he is released from hospital he will still be back and forth. After that another "stage" of treatment will start. We are hoping that he can start visiting his school in about six weeks and gradually build up over the months after to go back full time. Seth has a BIG fight on his hands for the next three years before he can start to live a disease free life.

What can you do? Please if you can, donate blood. That is the number one thing Seth will be relying on for platelets, plazma, bone marrow and the list goes on. Although the blood you donate won't directly go to Seth it will help other people and of course kids around the world.

Nikki, Holly and I are taking each hour as it comes and although it is not getting easier, we are constantly given direction from all the staff at Monash Medical Centre in Clayton and most importantly INFORMATION.

There is currently an 80-85% survival rate and WE are working at that! We are very lucky that it was diagnosed early and has not spread to his testis or spine :)

Thanks for all the messages of support we have already received and we will keep you up dated as we get through each stage.

Seth, Simon, Nikki and Holly

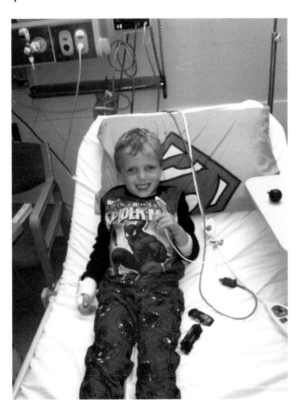

**18/05/12**

WOO BLOODY HOO!!!

This morning's blood test came back with great news!  His platelets were 100 or so yesterday, now they're 20 (We want 0) and although his haemoglobin (spell?) is low and he needs a plasma and blood transfusion today, it is expected!  So we are all walking around with a small smile on our faces. This afternoon after the transfusions he can go to the Cancer ward playroom and have a play and just when you think his smile can't get bigger.................IT DOES.

So with this response he is right on track to be in remission in about 3 1/2 weeks and even home as early as this Monday.

Thank you to everyone for ALL the support!!  A message, e-mails, phone calls, prays and the list goes on, as we now know they are working.

Simon, Nikki, Seth and Holly

*The information above is not correct. I took in so much information that I managed to mix it all up. Seth needed to be 0 with regard to Leukaemia cells (Blasts) not Platelets. Nikki and I didn't like watching the blood and other product transfusions. I think it was because we knew they were helping to keep our little boy live and we as parents couldn't fix it, we had to rely on strangers. Over time I was able to accept the transfusions, Nikki kept a smile on her face but had trouble with every single one.*

**19/05/12**

Hi,

Just a quick note...

All things that need to go down are doing that!!!

Blasts are what we need to be 0, not whatever it was I said yesterday that were at 8 yesterday, they are at 4 today.

I think its platelets that need to be 10ish and they're 8 so that's brilliant!!

Simon, Nikki, Seth and Holly

**25/05/12**

Hello, hi and G'day!

Seth is now HOME!!!!!!!

More blood tests on Monday, maybe a visit to hospital for a transfusion Monday or Tuesday and definitely his weekly Chemo Wednesday, BUT HE'S HOME!!!!

Please if you want to visit, we'd all love to see you, but if you have even a sniffle please wait until you're better.  His immune system is basically nonexistent and he will not be able to defend any bugs so it will mean being re-admitted into hospital and having an IV drip, so please think of his requirements when visiting.......................................it doesn't take long for you to get over a cold.

Simon, Nikki, Seth & Holly

*Packing up his hospital room was mixed emotions. We knew he was fighting for his life but we were on our way home because he was well enough. I'd read a lot of information by this time and had a*

4

*better understanding of what his body was not only going through, but what it needed to do with the drugs that were being injected. The car ride home was exciting, eager for him to get back into his room, eager for him to see his dog Astro that is almost to the day 1 year older than him and would become his companion throughout treatment. Astro slowed down a lot when Seth was not home in the coming years. He'd sleep in Seth's room waiting for him, he'd go to the door whenever he heard a noise and then his tail would wag and wag and wag and he'd become Seth's shadow when he did come home. Seth wanted to see his cat, Puss Puss. Puss Puss was 15 and lived in the laundry. Seth spent many hours in the coming years talking, patting and checking up on Puss Puss. Unfortunately before treatment ended, Puss Puss passed away in his sleep about a month before his 17th birthday. Then there is Seth's fish, he was worried that they weren't looked after. In the coming months Seth was given a bigger tank and we started to get it ready for tropical fish, rather than gold fish. Seth spent many hours watching his fish swim around, he found it to be relaxing. When Seth arrived home, he walked around our house so many times, looking, checking, trying to see if anything had changed in the few weeks he was away. Then we sat in our home as a family fighting Leukaemia and had dinner and watched something on TV that would've been Seth's choice. Holly and Astro fought over who would be closer to him, they both worked out that he needed to go to the toilet alone, but even in the shoer they were there... Holly was 13 months old when Seth was diagnosed.*

## 29/05/12

Hi all,
Seth had a fantastic weekend at home!
He had a blood test yesterday and as we haven't heard from the hospital, the results must be good and we will trek back there Wednesday for another Lumbar Puncture, Bone Marrow test and chemo. He is still really cheeky and happy and just wants to go to school and play on the playground. We are hoping he can go back at the start of term 3.
Simon, Nikki, Seth and Holly

*Any child under 18 has Lumbar Punctures, Bone Marrow extraction etc under general anaesthetic. The team at the hospital chat to the children while being wheeled into the room and then they pick a "smell" to be rubbed into the gas mask so the smell is manageable, then needles etc are inserted once they're asleep. Some operations were over in under 45 minutes, others took hours. It didn't matter how long they were, it was too long for him to be away from us.*

## 29/05/12

Hi everyone!!!
Tomorrow Seth will have a Bone Marrow operation to see how the medication is going. He does not need a lumbar puncture or blood transfusion. A blood transfusion is required if they are 80 or less and yesterdays result is 97 :)
All the messages, prayers, time at home etc. is working a treat!
Bring on remission day 28 - 12/06/12.
Simon, Nikki, Seth and Holly

## Chapter 2

**04/06/12**

Hi,

Seth is in really good spirits and we've had another week and weekend at home which is brilliant! The bone marrow results from last Wednesday still haven't come through, but the specialist said Seth is not quite as close to remission as they'd like, but he's still fighting. Today he had a blood test and generally he is ok, but some levels are low and he is very open to picking up a bug or infection easily.

We hope to hear more tomorrow before we go to the hospital on Wednesday for more chemo.

Simon, Nikki, Seth and Holly

**05/06/12**

Hi everyone,

Thanks again for all the cards, messages, prayers, food etc ... we are so overwhelmed by the support!!!

Well, Seth scared the shit out of me last week (excuse my French). He was not progressing as well as he should have been and the word "transplant" was one word thrown across the table at one point. He had a bone marrow test last Wednesday and the results for some reason were not processed until late yesterday afternoon and I got a message from the specialist in bone marrow saying "I need to talk with Seth's Oncologist, but don't worry things are ok". Simon being Simon started to panic again. Well keep your prayers and messages etc coming because he is now under 5% in his Bone Marrow and has a high probability of being in remission next week. 12/06/12 is day 28, we will be off to the hospital for a few tests to see where he is at on day 29.....Wednesday so keep positive and hopefully in less than 2 weeks we will be celebrating that he's in remission!

Anyway, chemo again tomorrow.

Simon, Nikki, Seth and Holly

*We were about 3 weeks since diagnosis. I'd started back at work, Nikki had resigned and Holly was no longer going to crèche. We had adapted our life and were getting used to it pretty quickly. I was Seth's biggest threat for infection because I was in public the most, but keeping hands clean etc helped him stay safe. We made his room a "rest" area. Whenever we had visitors, if he was tired he'd go into his room to rest and we asked our visitors to not follow him. This also helped to keep his room free from infection. Seth hadn't visited his school yet and we were filling out paperwork constantly. It was hospital forms (later we agreed to a trial drug and more forms were signed for the Boston Hospital), school forms, children's cancer charity forms... There's that Cancer word next to children again... I had all sorts of trouble getting used to that!*

**13/06/12**

G'day,

Seth had his op this morning and is on his way home. All went as well as can be expected and I am sure he's REALLY happy not to have Chemotherapy today. Now we wait until Tuesday which is when we will get the results and then be given his next plan of treatment and Thursday he needs to go in and have a "line" put in which is a thingy that sits under his skin at the bottom of his rib cage and a tube goes under his rib cage up to one of the major veins in his neck. This is done so he won't be such a pin cushion and any blood tests, chemotherapy, IV's etc can be put through that.

Thanks for all your messages!!!! Seth gets a kick out reading them.

Simon, Nikki, Seth and Holly

**18/06/12**

### HE'S IN REMISSION!

Hi all,

Seth had to visit the E.D. at the Monash Sat and Sun night as he has a temperature and required antibiotics. Luckily he has come home each night. As a follow up, Nikki, Holly and my Mum have taken him to the Children's Cancer Centre (our 2nd home) so he can have a full check up by the Dr's that are part of his case. Seth's Oncologist wasn't meant to be working there today and we have an appointment with her tomorrow, well she is there today and she is such a heartfelt wonderful woman because she told Nikki that Seth's results are back and they are negative!!!

Tomorrow we will find out about the next stage of treatment, but THANK YOU for all your prayers, messages, love etc...............HE DID IT!!!

Simon, Nikki, Seth and Holly

*I was at work and had arranged to work from home the next day so I could go and find out with Nikki and Holly if Seth was in remission or what was involved with a Bone Marrow Transplant because the Chemo wasn't working. The phone rang and I thought I would here Seth on the other end telling me they were on their way to the car to go home. I heard Nikki's voice. It was quieter than normal and I had trouble understand but I feared the worst, I thought she was trying to tell me that Seth had to start 6 weeks of intense chemo while a Bone Marrow donor was found. Then I heard her say "Seth is negative", I asked her to tell me what that meant, with a burst of energy and tears stopped for a few seconds, I heard "Seth is in remission, he did it". I burst into tears, uncontrollable happy tears. My work colleague couldn't help but hear my end of the conversation and as I hung up the phone and turned to him, he had his head in his hands and was crying too. He thought Seth was in trouble. I couldn't talk all I could do was hold 2 thumbs up. Apparently he saw the biggest smile he'd ever seen in amongst the red eyes and tears. I managed to talk after a few minutes and then went to tell my boss. AGAIN!!!! Tears poured out and he panicked, I could see in his face and so I held up 2 thumbs again and he was instantly relieved. I know we chatted for a while, all I remember is him asking why I hadn't left to be with my family yet, that was a very happy, music up flat out 45 minute drive home!*

## Chapter 3

**02/07/12**

Hi Everyone,

Where do I start?

Today Seth had Chemo via his port and then had a "butterfly" put on his leg and then Chemo through that (he needs that 4 days in a row and it needs to go into fat tissue which is why his port isn't used) and then because he doesn't quite glow in the dark, I just gave him more Chemo (tablet dissolved in water) here at home.

Tomorrow, Wednesday and Thursday a nurse will come and inject Chemo via the butterfly and remove it after Thursday's treatment. Tablets go for 14 days. Next week is a lumber puncture and more Chemo via his port.............NO BLOODY STEROIDS YET :)

Slowly he is losing weight, still about 5 & 1/2-6kg's to get back to pre diagnosis weight, but he is feeling a lot happier when he looks in the mirror now.

All the Chemo this and next week will knock him about and Nikki and I were warned that he'll most likely be admitted to hospital next week because of it.................they have said that before and he hasn't so we hope he isn't, but at least we know it's a strong possibility.

Simon, Nikki, Seth and Holly

**25/07/12**

Hi,
Seth is doing really well with Radiation Therapy and still hasn't used a general anaesthetic, today we met with his Dr at Peter Mac and was amazed how well he copes and that he doesn't need a G.A.

*Radiation sort of snuck up on us. We had forgotten about it until Nikki read some paperwork and then we were off to Peter Mac in the city. Seth had to have a mask made and then set it up on the bed for when we'd go back so the radiation was accurate and precise to where it need to go. This is because the human body is protective of the spine and brain. Medication has difficulty crossing into these areas. Seth has T-Cell Leukaemia and one of the areas known commonly for relapse is in the brain but a specific area of the brain. The radiation is used to kill the brain cells in that area to lessen the likely hood of relapse.*

**27/07/12**

Hi,
Today Seth, Holly and Nikki are on their way to see me at work for a late lunch.
He has had day 5 of 8 radiation therapies and is doing it with a small screen in front of him with Ben 10 and NO anaesthetic.
Next Monday, Tuesday and Wednesday he has the last of that treatment.
The week after is now moved from the Royal Children's to the Monash which although he enjoys the Children's, he is happier within his environment at the Children's Cancer Centre.
Simon, Nikki, Seth and Holly!

## Chapter 4

**02/08/12**

Hi,

There is no words, just feelings, tingles, numbness..........Seth is doing really well and is also really accepting that he may not be back at school this year, an hour here and there is about all. I have done some stuff and seen some stuff; my hero is my 5 1/2 year old son.

Today he went on his scooter and it's made me a bit emotional, but for a long time now I really do see him as my hero. He knows he's sick, he knows the radiation will make him feel sick and maybe vomit, he knows the chemo will make him feel sick, maybe make him vomit and will also put him at risk of infection and hospitalisation and after knowing all of that, after feeling all of that, he walks in to get his treatment with a smile, he walks out after his treatment with a smile... why?... because he wants to get better and he knows that smiling helps.

Simon

*I wrote this after reflecting, thinking, dreaming of a cure, hoping he can win this fight, hoping we can beat this fight. It was also little comments Seth made, the way the mask looked, the way it looked when he was on the table of the machine and it was screwed into position...*

I am not a monster!

My name is Seth and I am 5 1/2 years old.

I have (ALL) Leukaemia and as part of my treatment I needed to have 8 radiation treatments.

I had all 8 of my treatments without anaesthetic.

Lots of people from the hospital and even a friend of my Dad from the other side of Australia whom is a nurse are amazed because adults apparently sometimes need anaesthetic.

I don't like being in the room by myself, but the radiographer let me pick something to watch while I'm there.

There are cameras in the room so I know I'm safe, but I also have a bell in my hand just in case.

I didn't use it. I just did what I was asked to do and watched Ben 10 when they left me in the room while I had my treatment.

Mum & Dad told me that the quicker I do as I'm asked the quicker we can do something fun like go to the park, lucky it didn't rain much during those 8 days because I can't go into public much......the chemotherapy I had the week before makes it easy for me to get infections.

The mask doesn't hurt, it's just annoying.

My name is Seth and I am 5 1/2 years old.

I am not a monster!

*You're about to see a pic of Seth in the mask on the table about to have radiation. You can see the lines projected onto the mask that line up with marks on the mask to make it accurate. You can also see that the mask needed padding. In between him having the mask fitted to him and treatment started, he lost a lot of the weight he'd gain whilst on steroids.*

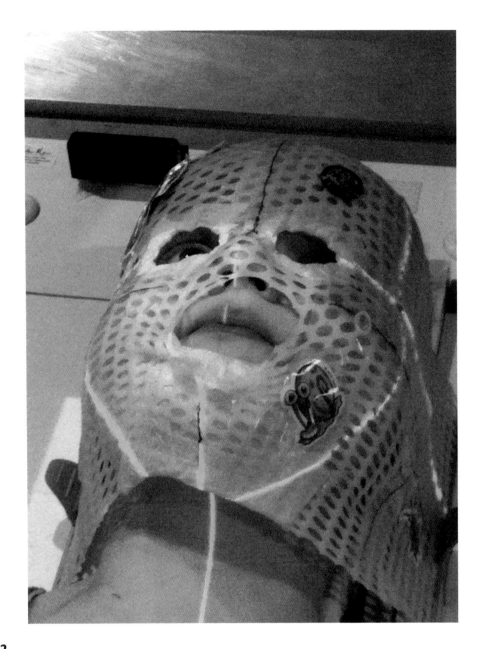

**08/08/12**

G'day, hi and HELLO,

Seth has a bit of a runny nose that has slowed things down this week; well he now has a week off treatment.

BUMMER - Seth's neutrophil count is still slightly too low to begin chemo. Neutrophil's are what fights infection. They also cannot be transfused, so we will go back next week and start this week's treatment as long as he's got rid of his runny nose and they've had a chance to recover.

Interesting fact: Normal count 5 year old is 1.8-7.7. Operations and chemo cannot be done unless 0.75 or higher. Seth is 0.55.

Ultimately there is nothing to worry about, Seth's general health is strong and the specialist's would admit him to hospital if there was any issue.  It just means that he needs to be isolated again from risk of further infection and somehow we need to find a way to get him to rest so he can recover.

Simon, Nikki, Seth and Holly

**13/08/12**

Hi,

I just got a call from Nikki whom is with Seth at the Monash Medical Centre.  All systems are go, his levels are high enough to go ahead with this week's chemotherapy.

Seth will be having chemo at the Monash daily this week and the treatment takes approx 2 hours, BUT it takes an hour to make it and the pharmacists won't until he's there.

Also it is given 24 hours apart, so he'll be getting it approx 1pm each day so he'll be tired by the end of the week.  Today is also 3 months (13/05/12) since he went with Nikki

to the E.D. department and ultimately admitted the next day and confirmation of Leukaemia a few days later.

WELL DONE SETH, WE'RE ALL DOING THIS WITH YOU MATE!!!

Simon, Nikki, Seth and Holly

**21/08/12**

Hi,

Seth is doing really well with his treatment and he has even had some of his hair grow back :)

On Friday at the school assembly the principal is giving Seth an ipad with pre-paid internet, apps, Skype and also an iTunes voucher.

A few weeks ago they did a fundraiser and raised the money in four days. The aim is to be able to keep his education going and to take some of the home school stress off Nikki by way of him Skyping his class and joining in when he can't go there. It will also help his class mates understand what Seth does because he will show them around his room at home as well as when he goes for chemo at the hospital he'll show them around the Children's Cancer Centre.

Nikki just had a call from his school. The local Leader newspaper wants Nikki to contact them and give permission for them to come to the assembly and take photo's and write a story about Seth and how his school is helping him. Now he's going to be famous because his school has been incredible and to get this sort of free widespread coverage I think is brilliant for the school and ultimately Leukaemia awareness as there is more kids diagnosed in this area than any other area in Melbourne due to the amount of growth between here and Pakenham.

Also, Camp Quality is going to his school on Thursday and is showing 4 puppet shows to all the students and teachers. The shows are age appropriate and will help them understand what Seth (and others) is going through while he's not at school. It also explains why he "comes and goes" and why his hair falls out etc. A primary school with 500 kids and they do this for Seth, I still can't believe how many people he knows and how supportive his school really is.

Simon, Nikki, Seth & Holly

*The ipad was an amazing gift from the school community. Seth Skyped his class (Skype is sort of a video phone call via the internet. It is live and he can see his class and they can see him) a number of times. It was usually on Friday afternoon when the class had "Fruit and Story". Each time some of the kids had an opportunity to ask Seth a question and Seth would show them around his hospital room or bedroom, depending on where he was. I don't remember the date, but I remember Seth had been away from school lot and so his teacher organised to Skype from the whole school assembly. I was at work and Nikki was in hospital with Seth. I got a phone call from one of the Dads. He was almost in tears because he said that the school tried to hook up the computer to a screen so Seth could be seen by everyone, but it didn't work. Instead he sat on his teachers lap with his class but the tears were tears of joy! He told me that after they couldn't surprise the students with Seth on the screen, they announced he was on Skype and could see and hear them... The hall nearly had its roof blown off from the noise, I was told that it was so loud, parents had to cover their ears. Nikki later told me that the speaker on the ipad distorted and they couldn't hear anything. Seth was scared to go to school because he had lost his hair and put on weight. Camp Quality took their puppet show and everyone throughout the day sat and watched, sat and learnt why Seth was different to when he was at school in term 1. When he went for a visit so many kids told him about the puppets and that they were so glad to see him at school.*

## Chapter 5

**14/09/12**

Hi,

Yesterday marked four months since Seth was taken to emergency. I know its "flown by", but it's been a long time for us. Some of you already know that Seth went to hospital for his last chemo treatment for this round on Wednesday. He has a few weeks off and then the next round/stage starts and it will be alot easier for that stage in regard to him and his treatment
before it steps up again to be intense and that stage will most likely take us into the New Year. Seth had a temp on Wednesday and after his chemo treatment he was admitted into hospital. He was hoping to come home tonight, but unfortunately at night his temp rises so it's likely he will have his antibiotics changed and be in hospital all weekend and maybe early next week. Blood tests have been done and they are working out what sort of infection he has picked up so then they can use a specific antibiotic rather than a broad one. The main reason he is not coming home is because his Neutrophil's are below 1 so he has not got any immunity to any infection, maybe if they were higher he could come home and be monitored,
so keep your fingers crossed that the temp lowers and the Neutrophil's start lifting so he can come home ASAP.

Message from Seth:
"Do you think because it's the weekend if my friends aren't sick their Mum and Dad might bring them into see me?"
So if your kids are healthy and haven't had a runny nose or cough for at least 7 days please see if you can squeeze in an hour to come down and see Seth. It is a long day when you can't do much so some visitors would definitely be appreciated by him.
Have a great weekend,
Simon, Nikki, Seth and Holly
P.S. Seth is on page 12, Berwick Leader, 10/09/12.....again a massive thank you to his principal Mr Williams, his teacher Miss Berryman
and all at his school!!!!!!!!!!!!!

**18/09/12**

Hi,

Seth is on his way home from hospital now. He spent 6 nights waiting for his blood to build immunity back up. He hasn't had a temp since Friday. He is still talking about his Skype chat last Friday and it seems that all his class mates are too because Jacob and James came to see him over the weekend and that's all they seemed to talk about, well a little about Mighty Beans too :)

Have a great week!!
Simon

## Chapter 6

**3/10/12**

Hi,

I just got home from work to find out that Seth's neutrophil are at 0.44 and need to be at 0.75 before chemo can start again.  So he has another week to wait and see, on the positive he was 0.18 last week so his little body is doing it's best to get up there.

Don't forget we prefer him to be over 1, but "normal" 5 year olds range between 3 and 7.

Simon, Nikki, Seth and Holly

**10/10/12**

Hi,

WOW what a month!!  Yes, it is a month tomorrow (Wednesday) since Seth's last chemo treatment.  His Neutrophil's are up so tomorrow's lumbar puncture, bone marrow extraction and IV chemo is going ahead!

This treatment is the start of the next stage and is going to be relatively easy on his body.  The next stage is expected to be horrible.

From,

Simon, Nikki, Seth & Holly

**18/10/12**

G'day,

Seth is doing really well so far with this stage of treatment and went to school
Friday and yesterday for just over an hour each day.  He has also managed to
balance his weight at the moment which means he doesn't need a feeding tube
at this stage :)

Simon, Nikki, Seth & Holly

**21/10/12**

Hi all,

We missed a call from the Children's Cancer Centre yesterday afternoon (they normally only call the night before an operation), but the message was that Seth's chemo is going ahead today as planned and his Neutrophil's are at 8!!

If you don't remember, a normal 5 year old boy ranges between 3 and 7 and last week he was 3.45.  This is FANTASTIC news because his body is doing a better job than expected and after this treatment stage concludes, the next is really going to take its toll on him and his body.  We have already been advised that he is most likely going to need to be admitted to hospital for a week or more during that stage.  That stage will start about early December and take us to about early February, then we will be at about the 9 month mark and his treatment will slowly be decreased and he will be able to start getting back to an almost normal life with school (part time), seeing his mates, even going to shopping centres whenever he wants to.  Early evening we are going to Phillip Island for 2 nights with Camp Quality, so I'll take some pics and let you know what we experienced and tell you first hand where the money that charities make goes.  Have a great weekend!

Simon, Nikki, Seth & Holly

## Chapter 7

**1/11/12**

Hi everyone!

Seth is having chemo now as I write. His Neutrophil's have dropped to just over 2, this is an expected side effect of the chemo treatment he's having at the moment. He had a head cold last week and this morning his nose is a little runny again, Holly has an ear and throat infection as well as Hand Foot Mouth disease (luckily Seth hasn't caught it) and is coping really well with the horrible blisters. I have a throat infection and energy is affected. His oncologist has said that he can go to school on Wednesday afternoon for "buddy time" and he is REALLY looking forward to going.

Seth has asked for jokes, he always asks me for new kid jokes and I'm running out so if you know any good kid jokes please let me know so I can tell them to him.

Seth also asked me to write "HI FROM SETH" next time I told our friends about his progress. :)

Simon, Nikki, Seth and Holly

**8/11/12**

Hi,

We're one treatment (next Friday) away from the completion of this stage of treatment. Today Seth had a lumber puncture and then more chemo via his port and YAY they're home before 3pm :)

Nikki just took a call from "Starlight Foundation" and Seth, Holly and Nikki have been invited to Santa's arrival concert Saturday morning in Burke St Mall. It is a free event, but they will be at the front in a reserved area.

Then the phone rang again and Nikki took a call from "Challenge" and Seth, Holly, Nikki and I are off to Burnley oval next Thursday night for the opening of Santa's Magical Kingdom and we will meet the CEO of Challenge too.

We are trying to get all Christmassy early this year as again today we were reminded of what to expect from mid December.

My little idol, my little hero is doing really well and loved everyone's jokes. His fave was -

What's invisible and smells like carrots?

A rabbit fart.

Simon, Nikki, Seth & Holly

**12/11/12**

Hi,

Yesterday Seth started Milo Cricket. It is designed for 5-8 year olds. It goes for 8 weeks, 4 this side and 4 the other side of Christmas. He loved it!

It has a $75 joining fee to pay for t-shirt/hat/bat/ball/back pack. Anyway, the club contacted Cricket Australia (they run it) to see if the fee could be waived, otherwise the club was going to pay it for Seth because we don't think he'll be well enough after Christmas to go.

Cricket Australia waived the fee and sent the "area" representative out to meet Seth. After a few participations/rests the morning was over and Seth had a few pics taken so that the people at the office can put a face to the name.......in his cricket gear of course.

Today the rep e-mailed me asking if Cricket Victoria could do an interview for their website. Tonight at 7.30pm a lady is calling home to interview Nikki and I over the phone.

Again, I find myself asking "why Seth, why us?" I have found my answer, and it is simple.....We want to help other families, lots don't, that's why "our Seth" is helping others!!!

Simon

**17/11/12**

This is online at: http://www.cricketvictoria.com.au/news/article/there-s-no-stopping-seth

**Five-year-old leukaemia patient Seth Sleep recently found a new hobby to smile about - cricket!**

After attending his first MILO in2CRICKET session last Sunday at Narre Warren South Cricket Club, Seth told his father that "cricket was fun and he couldn't wait to go again (next) Sunday."

On Mother's Day this year, the Sleep family's life changed dramatically as Seth was diagnosed with T-Cell acute lymphoblastic leukaemia.

For parents Simon and Nikki, life would now consist of watching their son being poked and prodded by physicians.

"We are so proud of him," Mrs Sleep said.

"They (the doctors) say do something and he just does it."

After being housebound for the majority of six months, Seth was enrolled into the MILO in2CRICKET program to higher his confidence; allow him to socialise with other children and to keep him strong and active.

"He has the chance to run around and let energy go," Mrs Sleep said.

"Hopefully this can have a positive effect on his treatment."

Later this month, Seth will be the 13th man for the Commonwealth Bank Bushrangers during their RYOBI One-Day Cup match against South Australia.

Along with Cricket Victoria and Cricket Australia, organisations including Camp Quality, Challenge, Starlight and Red Kite have shown their support for the Sleep family, organising activities and lending a hand financially.

The Trinity Catholic Primary School community have also thrown their support behind the Sleep family, providing Seth with an ipad to keep in touch with his classmates.

"We have just been overwhelmed by the generosity shown by everyone," Mrs Sleep said.

For the next three years, Seth will undergo a numerous amount of chemotherapy, blood and platelet transfusions and will face the chance of relapse until he is officially diagnosed as being 'cured'.

"The reality is that it's an uncertain future for us and no parent ever wants to go through that," Mrs Sleep said.

14 NOVEMBER, 2012|Sarah Carpinteri | Game Development

**20/11/12**

Hi all,

Seth has now completed this stage of treatment! He is still doing an amazing job with understanding why and that sometimes he can't go into public or to a birthday party etc. due to his blood levels or general energy etc.

THIS WEEK MARKS SIX MONTHS! 13/05/12 is when he went to the ED and Leukaemia was confirmed by (if not before) 17/05/12.

Seth started Milo In2 Cricket last Sunday and loves it. He has 2 classmates doing it too. Aaron Dragwidge from Cricket Australia took time out of his Sunday to come and see the club and have a photo with Seth. He then contacted Cricket Victoria and all going well Seth will be the 13th man on the Victorian Bushrangers side at the MCG 28/11/12. He will be in their t-shirt and hat and toss the coin; apparently as it is "Ryobi Cup" it will also be televised on Fox Sports....The game starts at 2.15pm.

Also the local cricket club (Narre South Cricket Club) is buying him some cricket shoes and getting him his own one day jumper with "SLEEPY" and the number "7" on it.

He has also been to school for a few hours a couple of times this week and comes home absolutely exhausted, but with a BIG smile on his face.

19

Last night we went to Santa's Magical Kingdom with CHALLENGE - helping kids live with cancer and we all loved it! Bedtime is normally 7.30 and both kids were still "buzzing" at 9pm when we got in the car. A highly recommended thing to do if you can.

Seth's next treatment stage goes for approximately nine weeks and will be very intensive! As I've said before, we have been warned that he may be admitted to hospital over Christmas and New Year. We are waiting on time and blood tests, but that will start in 2-3 Wednesdays.

Please have a look at the story about Seth and cricket, you'll also find it on
www.cricketvictoria.com.au
http://www.cricketvictoria.com.au/news/article/there-s-no-stopping-seth

Have a great weekend,
Simon, Nikki, Seth and Holly

## 23/11/12

Hi all,
This week, WOW what a week.
Saturday my best mate 40th was on and Nikki went to a Christmas Lunch in Yering so we dropped her off and went to Mooroolbark to set up for a big night. Then the phone rang and the birthday boy's brother in-law had blown up his car and needed help. This was FANTASTIC because off I went to help my mate and his family with their car with Holly in tow and the birthday boy shot off to Yering to pick Nikki up while Seth stayed behind at the house to play with the kids. He has really formed a security blanket around himself with Nikki and I and it was so nice to be able to leave him playing with his friends. (And I didn't get a chance to even have one drink with the birthday boy)
Sunday Seth had Milo In2 Cricket in the morning. It got rained out after about half an hour, so off to the club rooms for a sausage in bread and some fruit. After cricket I had a Mitsubishi Pajero lo lose control and try to drive into the driver's door of my work car.......ouch!!!
Seth had a blood test for platelet levels yesterday and YAY!!!! No transfusion required today.
Today Seth's Poppy spoke about him and his treatment on community radio in Ballarat, with great success (99.9 Voice FM).
Tomorrow is one of his cousin's birthday parties and he can't wait to get there. Sunday is cricket (If treatment starts Wednesday we expect this to be his last to participate) and then a birthday party for a class mate and then a birthday party for one of the kids rescued last weekend, OH and an outdoor movie tonight with Camp Quality.
Tuesday Seth will have another blood test to check "everything" in preparation for a chemo lumber puncture operation and then more via IV afterwards on Wednesday. If this happens it means that his treatment has started one week early. It also means he won't be able to go and be the 13th man with the Bush Rangers at the "G". Cricket Victoria have offered Seth the opportunity to be the 13th man on either the 13th or 16th of February next year if he can't make it this time.
I have also found out that Seth has been invited to meet the players of Melbourne Stars at their family day on the 9/12/12.
Seth will also not be able to go back to school for classes this year if the treatment starts Wednesday as the side effect will make him unable, except for a short visit.

Have a great weekend,
Simon, Nikki, Seth and Holly

**27/11/12**

Hi,

This week Seth is not ready for chemo to start.  It was decided that he shouldn't be brought forward one week and his Neutrophil's are 0.59, treatment will not commence until they are over 0.70.

So, Seth will be the 13th man for the Victorian Bushrangers at the MCG tomorrow (Wednesday 28th).  I don't have Foxtel; apparently it is a Ryobi Cup game so it will be on Fox Sport.  I don't expect him to last more than a few hours.

Nikki and I also had a phone interview with the Herald Sun and they sent a photographer to our place to take pics for the article.  This is expected to go to print Wednesday 28th, but if they don't have "space" it will be printed within the next few days.  (A BIG thanks to Aaron from Cricket Aus. for taking time to come over while the photos were being taken and then giving Seth some brilliant batting tips, so good he showed them off to the seniors training at the cricket club tonight).

I am working Saturday morning, so Nikki is taking Seth and Holly to the "Challenge" Christmas party at Sandown Race course and then we are off to the city because Seth was given tickets from "Starlight Foundation" to see the Wiggles in the afternoon.  Sunday is his last In2 Cricket session for this year.

Lets hope his platelets stay high and his Neutrophil's lift so it will be safe for him to be able to do everything this weekend.

Have a great week,
Simon, Nikki, Seth and Holly

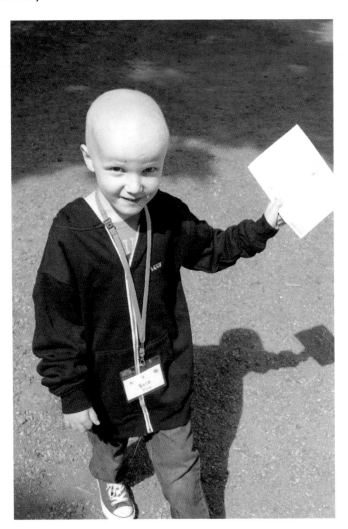

21

## Chapter 8

**4/12/12**

Hi

Tonight the hospital called and Seth is starting the next treatment stage tomorrow morning.
He had an absolute blast as 13th man for the Bushrangers at the "G" and this Sunday he is
going to meet the Melbourne Stars including Sir Viv Richards, Shane Warne, Cameron White
(again) and Malinga along with 1000 other lucky kids before the gates open to the general
public at a family day.
That's going to be the last time he will probably be able to do anything outside the house this
year.  So it's time to get out "Grandpa in my pocket" and "Ben 10" again to keep him sane.
Thank you all for your wonderful messages and support via e-mail, Facebook and phone.
You really are all special to us and as I am quickly finding out that you all have VERY big hearts!

Simon, Nikki, Seth and Holly

P.S. Seth has taken to cricket at an amazing rate of knots and Cricket Aus. and Cricket Vic. along
with Narre South Cricket Club are helping him so much, it really is incredible that even when he's
tired, he fights us to stay because he's having so much fun!  THANK YOU.

**14/12/12**

Hi all,
Seth is on his way home as I write to you.
Today he had chemo via IV (drip) for 2 hours and then observation for 4 hours and finally he has
been given the all clear and he and Nikki are on their way home.
He will also be back at the hospital for more chemo Wednesday afternoon.  Yesterday we had the

pleasure of being a guest of the Melbourne Stars cricket team.

Seth was not himself (side effects well and truly kicked in) but we met the players and some recognised him from when he was 13th man for the Bushrangers a few weeks ago. He was VERY spoilt and given a Kookaburra bat with the whole team named and autographed on it. I got some "strange" looks from people while we were walking around the oval, it took a while to realise they were looking at the bat and not my shaved head :) I not only got to catch up with a few players we met at the G, but also meet Shane Warne and Sir Viv Richards which I watched as a kid, teenager, adult............AMAZING! Viv was so nice to everyone and I know Shane gets a lot of crap in the media but he was so nice to us, he even came back to get some photo's taken.

While Seth and I and he was very lucky to be able to take his mate James and Dave his Dad, Seth's club NARRE SOUTH CRICKET CLUB (our club I should say) were here doing a massive cleanup of our yard. They weeded, mulched, dug, trenched, laid agi and the list goes on. Seth and Holly were even given a swimming pool to get them through Summer because Seth can't risk infection using a public pool. I have also been told (SSHHHHHHHH don't tell Seth or Holly) that Santa is hoping to make an appearance at our place on Christmas Eve too.

We hope you all have a great week,
 Simon, Nikki, Seth and Holly

P.S. This e-mail is now going to a lot more people and the list is growing, don't forget that if you don't want to be on the list let me know and to the newbie's, WELCOME!

**19/12/12**

Hi everyone,
This afternoon as I write Seth is at the hospital having another round of chemo and about to start another week of steroids.
I know I've said it a million and one times, but Seth is my Super hero! He happily gets ready and hops into the car and off he goes to the hospital. When he gets there, he sometimes says hello, but always smiles and eventually makes sure he has had a chat with all the staff. Then he sits and watches the needle go in, watches everything get hooked up and then off he goes for another game

on his Nintendo DS or ipad.

We were warned at the start of this stage to expect a hospital admission and he (again) looks like he's going to show them that he doesn't want to go to hospital so he won't get sick (I hope I haven't spoken too soon). He has a friend named Aaron and he has decided that when he's cured and he can play proper cricket, Aaron will probably want to watch and then have a sausage after the game (Aaron is the man in the photo with Seth from the first week he went to In2 Cricket and it was put on Cricket Victoria's website).

He also asked me last night why he couldn't train with the boys at Narre South Cricket Club (Our club) on Tuesday nights and just watch. I told him that Mick didn't want him to show off to the boys and beat them. His response was priceless "Dad, I'm not silly, but you are! All you had to say was that I am not big enough yet".

He's about half way and going strong and really looking forward to giving Holly her Christmas present he bought her.....and don't forget about the big guy in a red suit for him too.

From Nikki, Seth, Holly and myself we wish you a brilliant Christmas and a fantastic New Year!

## Chapter 9

# <u>2013</u>

**3/01/13**

Hi all,

We got our bestest Christmas present ever!!!!  We ALL slept in our own beds and woke up together Christmas morning.  Seth and Holly had a FANTASTIC Christmas!!!  Santa came to visit and give them presents on Christmas Eve with thanks to the Narre South Cricket Club members, family and their friends buying them presents and then they woke up Christmas morning to discover he'd been back :) Boxing Day morning Seth had his last steroid tablet for this treatment........he's gained about 5kg the poor bugger.  So he doesn't have any more chemo this year :)  He's back to Monash on 2/01/13 to start chemo again and has 5 days, so we'll be going there on Saturday and Sunday too.  He has had a few temperature changes and we called the hospital Christmas night, but he hasn't needed to go back!

The bonus with his weight gain is that with the next month of treatment he will lose weight, so hopefully he will balance out and not drop so much that a feeder tube starts being thought about again.

So, a big HAPPY NEW YEAR to everyone and remember to ask why you're not smiling because Seth is :)

Simon, Nikki, Seth & Holly


**7/01/13**

Hi all,

Seth's favourite sandwich is ham cut off the bone on seeded bread, preferably pumpkin seed, and butter......he's having that today!!!

I just got a call from Nikki to say that Seth's Neutrophil's are at 0.91 so he is still neutropenic, but can start chemo after this three week break.

He has chemo every day this week, so they'll be off to the Monash and back each day as he doesn't need to be admitted.  This is the first week of his last four weeks for this stage so just like you all did at Christmas and kept him home, please cross fingers and toes, pray, give good energy thoughts etc. that this stage will now continue without another break.  Why, because if it continues it is looking like he won't have chemo at all the week of his birthday and although the hospital and charities like Koala Kids make birthdays extra enjoyable in hospital, there's no place like home :)  So let's all wish that he's home on the 14th of February for his 6th birthday and while we're at it I hope he's home so I get a birthday cuddle for my birthday the day before.

He hasn't told me any new jokes this year, but when he does I'll pass them onto you all.

Cricket has become his love and with this treatment his body, especially muscles will get knocked around and his favourite "Milo In2 Cricket" starts back on the 13th of January at his club, Narre South Cricket Club, and he won't be able to participate BUT we hope we can put him in the push bike trailer and trek down (for those that don't know, we need to do a marathon of 4 houses, one street, one more house and we're at the boundary fence of the club).

So for this week, we hope you have a great one!

Simon, Nikki, Seth and Holly

**17/01/13**

Hi,

Seth got through five continuous days of going back and forth to Monash Clayton for chemo last week. Saturday night we went to one of Seth's mates from school and cricket's house for a catch up and for him to release some tension and be an almost normal nearly six year old boy again. James also has a sister, Olivia that Holly adores and spent most of the night being her shadow. Sunday we had a really BIG bonus of being able to not only go to Milo In2 Cricket, but he participated for most of it and Mushy, a senior player gave him some practice in the nets before hand, along with a few other In2 Cricket kids. His treatment was moved from Monday to Wednesday so that he could have his lumber puncture in the Children's Cancer Centre rather than on the hospital emergency list. This is great because we know exactly what time he starts his op and don't have to wait if there's been a car accident etc to delay it. Also it meant that we were able to go to the Renegades V Heat Big Bash 20/20 as guests of Cricket Victoria. Seth got a few autographs on his top, had a couple of conversations with Jayde Herrick and Michael Hill and to top it off, a quick chat to Dane Swan from his much loved Collingwood Magpies footy team. Although Renegades lost, Seth had a great time and stayed to the last ball in case they won so he could see Michael, Jayde and the rest of the players in the rooms. Thankyou Cricket Victoria and especially Lauren Turner.

Wednesday he had his lumbar puncture and other chemo. He left home at 8am and got home STILL SMILING at 7pm. He did really well and had Aaron Dragwidge from Cricket Aus/Vic and Clive Rose from Melbourne Stars go see him for a few hours. Of all things to do and read in there, he played a game of Monopoly on the floor with them and I don't know who out of the three of them and Holly trying to join in had more fun or the biggest smile. Thanks Aaron and Clive.

Now each morning until Saturday a nurse comes to give him chemo through a "butterfly" in his leg which will be removed after his treatment on Saturday. He also has tablets to take for the next two weeks. Tomorrow (Friday) he's having some friends from school coming over to play in the afternoon.

We hope you are all keeping hydrated in the heat and remember to keep smiling,

Simon, Nikki, Seth and Holly

**24/01/13**

Hi,

This week has been hard on Seth's body. He had some mates over last Friday and it was so good to come home from work and see the house full of kids playing again. We went to the Drive In because he can't go into public enclosed areas like a cinema or supermarket etc, he said Wreck it Ralph was good, I was too busy chatting and taking turns with Nikki to try and keep Holly watching. Sunday he did most of the Milo In2 Cricket and then we went for a 5km bike ride in the afternoon. Tuesday night we all went to cricket training and he showed the boys how to warm up properly :) He also did his first push ups ever, not what you'd call a good push up, but he tried. Wednesday he had a lumbar puncture and more chemo at hospital and had it this morning at home via his "butterfly" in his leg. He is also taking chemo tablets each night that will stop Tuesday night. Friday he will have a blood test and then a blood transfusion as his blood levels are dropping. This is to be expected at this stage of his treatment. Next Wednesday will be the last chemo treatment for this stage and he'll have a few weeks off to recover. It will also mark a mile stone because it's the end of the most intensive treatment. Although it will still be hard on him, he'll be in "maintenance" so his hair will start to grow back, he'll be able to probably go back to school nearly full time in term 3 and the list goes on.

So happy Australia Day everyone and have a great weekend!

Keep smiling,

Simon, Nikki, Seth and Holly

*One thing you get used to is "missing out" on things. Friend's parties, BBQ's, gatherings... Nikki and I decided that on most occasions if Seth couldn't go, we all didn't go. We couldn't just jump in the car and go to the local shopping centre for a wander, the risk of the air conditioning, lack of fresh air ventilation etc is a breeding ground for infectious illnesses. A person with low immunity will almost certainly catch an infection if subjected to it. Movie theatres were out, supermarket, the local games arcade, anything enclosed was too risky. If someone gave Seth a voucher or money, we'd go to a shopping centre, but as soon as it opened before the air had been recirculated through the air con.*

**30/01/13**

Hi All,

As January 2013 gets closer to finishing, so does this stage of Seth's treatment :)

Last Friday he had a blood transfusion as his levels were getting low, which perked him up!

We did some more bike riding with Seth and Holly in the trailer as well as In2 Cricket on Sunday morning. He couldn't do much because he was lacking not only energy but also strength. Also Kathy Hempenstall from the Vic. Spirit - female cricket team came and gave all the kids some pointers on how to bowl and bat better which was great. Also on Sunday one of our neighbours organised for his uncle to come over with his new car he bought just before Christmas to take Seth for a joy ride. He didn't want to go in the bright red Ferrari, but his Dad did and WOW it is a lot of fun!!! On Monday Seth had a photo shoot for an article that's going into the Berwick Leader newspaper next week and then we went to his Nonna and Pa's to celebrate his Pa's birthday. We did a lot of rest and relaxation this week.

Today is Seth's last day of treatment for this stage so he'll have a few weeks off before another treatment plan starts. He and Nikki left home before 10am and are hoping to be home about 9pm. This is because he needs a platelet transfusion, one lot of chemo that takes a few minutes, another lot of chemo that takes 2 hours and then he needs to be observed for any side effects for 4 hours. Also his blood test taken yesterday and then confirmed by another blood test this morning has shown that he'll need a blood transfusion on Friday. HOPEFULLY that will be the last one for a while

27

and his body will recover enough to not need another next week.

It's now looking more likely that he'll be home and not having chemo on his birthday, BUT it is still a few weeks away so keep your fingers crossed! Due to his blood levels being low and requiring transfusions, unfortunately he won't be going to school for an hour on the first day back this Friday, BUT as soon as he's ready he'll be putting on his uniform and going to settle into grade 1.

Have a great rest of your week,

Keep smiling because as you know Seth is (and will be when he gets home sometime after 9 tonight)

Simon, Nikki, Seth & Holly.

## Chapter 10

**18/02/13**

Hi all,

What a month of February so for Seth!!

He officially finished the hardest 9 months of his life and with that the hardest part of his chemo.  On the 14th he turned 6 and had 3 friends from school and their brothers and sisters come around for Pizza and birthday cake.  Amanda from Amanda's Specialty Cakes also kept us big kids looked after with mini lemon meringues, mini Baileys cheesecakes and more yummy desserts.  Hopefully he can have a "real" birthday party in early March, at the moment his Neutrophil's are too low.  Yesterday the Narre South Cricket Club held a fundraiser for us.  Although it hit 37 degrees we all had a blast and so many people came and had heaps of fun on jumping castles and a big water slide etc.  Oh and of course there was a 20/20 big bash which is 20 over's per side and as many 4's and 6's as possible.  Booby Quiney, Michael Hill and Clive Rose came for a while to have pics, sign autographs and join in the fun of the day.  They all played for Victoria's Bushrangers on Saturday and again today so it is VERY appreciated that they came on their day off.  We also had the pleasure of Amberley Lobo, ABC3 presenter.  Kids came from everywhere and although it was hot, most wanted to give her a hug.  Tomorrow Seth has another blood test to check his levels as to whether he's ready to start "maintenance" chemo.  Once it starts he'll be in hospital for day visits for a few weeks and then one day a month and 5 days every 12 weeks.  He will also have chemo at home every day and steroids for one week every month.  The bestiestest news is that he will be able to start school for an hour or so a week either next week or the one after.  This will build up to hopefully nearly fulltime by term 4.  He also had another small step to cure last Saturday night; he had his hair washed by Nikki!!!!  Although it is basically fluff, it is covering his whole scalp so soon we'll be off to see Andrew at Andrews Barbershop in Beaconsfield for a hair cut!!!  He hasn't had hair since June 2012 and that was when he also had his last hair cut.  Seth still has 2&1/2 years of chemo, but he has achieved so much already.

So remember, if you're not smiling, why because Seth is.

Simon, Nikki, Seth & Holly

**25/02/13**

Hi,
I'll send a detailed update soon but, Seth went back to school today, he has now officially started grade 1!!!!
Simon

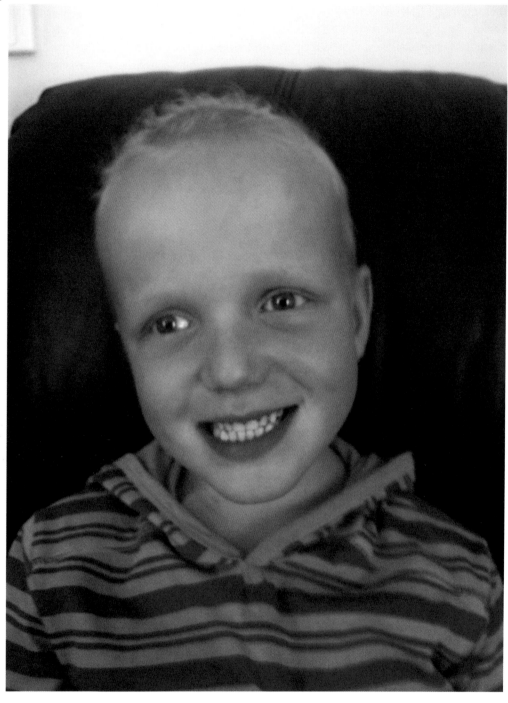

## Chapter 11

**5/03/13**

Good morning

Seth had a fantastic week at school last week, so fantastic he got a Principals award!!!!  We don't know what it was for because he didn't bring it home, but we will find out soon :)

He was also lucky enough to have another visit to the MCG and catch up with the Victorian Bushrangers and in his eyes, more importantly see Clive Rose, Michael Hill and Bobby Quiney....then he was also lucky enough to catch up with Jayde Herrick in the stand.  Unfortunately the Bushrangers lost the one day final, but that didn't matter to Seth.

He had a few birthday parties to go to over the last few weekends and I realised how much I'd missed the squeals and screaming that can only be heard at a kid's birthday party.  He also had his own party with his school mates and also received a "Smash Cake" from Naughty Nush and Koala Kids!!!!  His was an oversized cupcake made out of chocolate (like a big Easter egg) and filled with 500g of mixed lollies.  I'm not sure whether it was the kids or the grownups that enjoyed seeing it get smashed open, although it was a great way to get a little peace and quiet while the kids had a mouthful of lollies.

Just as the cricket season is coming to an end, Seth was admitted to hospital overnight.  Yesterday he wasn't his normal self and had a day off school.  By the time I got home from work Nikki had already spoken to the Children's Cancer Centre and a plan was in place............well his temp went up and down too much so off they went about 9pm last night.  At about 11pm he had a blood test and I.V. antibiotics had been started.  The results were rushed through and by midnight we knew he also needs a blood transfusion because his red blood cells are low.  So, about 3am he was admitted up on the ward and he will be there until at least tomorrow..........fingers crossed his Neutrophil's lift so he can come home and not spend too long in there.

He has his ipad so if you send a text to Nikki with a time, I am sure he'd love to "Skype" some friends to help pass time.

Have a great rest of the week and REMEMBER (he still is, even in hospital with tubes hooked up to him) If you're not smiling, why not because Seth is,

Simon, Nikki, Seth & Holly.

**18/03/13**

Hi Everyone,

Seth has had some fun the last couple of weeks.  He's been to school and had school photos.

He's been really good taking his chemo tablets everyday and his antibiotic as well.  Did I mention in the past that he has to have Bactrim (antibiotic) twice a day, 3 times a week whilst he is having chemo?  It is because he can get pneumonia very easily so the Bactrim "boosts" his body in the hope that when he gets a cold it doesn't develop.  Today he trekked back up to Monash Medical Centre in Clayton for chemo.  He now has chemo everyday at home and once a month he has to go to hospital for his clinical trial chemo and then another week he goes for a day or two for more chemo that needs to be administered through his port.  We are currently in the 10th month since diagnosis and he's doing really well.  So, what is the port?  It is a valve that is under his rib cage on the right side of his body.  It has a tube attached that goes up under his ribs into a vein in his neck.  All people in similar situations have this put in because the bodies veins collapse, this way they don't and also an anaesthetic cream is put over the access area so he also doesn't feel it.

What has he been doing?  He's been at the last cricket club training for the season and one of the Narre South Cricket Club teams, "D" won their premiership cup.  He's been at school and absolutely loving it!  OH, his Principal award was for - "A great start in grade 1.  He shows a positive attitude towards learning."  He hasn't been on his scooter at all or bike.  He's getting used to home work :)

He went with Ravi, someone he met through his T20 game on Saturday and helped shave his head

31

for "World's Greatest Shave", then in the afternoon we all did some laps at "Relay for Life" and Stuart, the organiser of the group we went to see did 62.8km's in 21 hours....AMAZING effort and he SMASHED last year's effort of 42Km's.  Yesterday we watched the planes fly over Albert Park Lake for the GP.

Friday we are hoping to get away for the weekend down to Blairgowrie, first time since pre diagnosis we've been able to go ............... keep your fingers crossed that we can get there and play on the beach and chill out a little too.

Have a great week,

and remember........IF YOU'RE NOT SMILING, WHY NOT BECAUSE SETH IS,

Simon, Nikki, Seth and Holly

**18/03/13**

Hi,

I just wanted to share a picture of Seth while he is getting chemo.  It's not so scary and he's still smiling.

I want to share this because I was once scared of chemo, cancer, hospital etc.  Seth has taught me to just get it done.

Nikki just posted this on Facebook -

"Day 1 of 5. Today is a long day for Seth, having a blood test, waiting for the results & then getting the ok. We have been here since 10 & chemo has just started we should be able to leave at about 3.30. The rest of the week should only be 2 hours each day. Seth is doing his favourite thing & colouring in some Easter drawings."

As you can see in the pic, there is no way to know he has chemo hooked up except I just told you. He doesn't feel pain and has nearly full mobility except for Mr Spaghetti.

Simon

**27/03/13**

Hi,

WE GOT DOWN TO BLAIRGOWRIE :)

Seth had chemo everyday at Monash last week and didn't go to school.  On Friday we all went there and after his treatment we headed off to Blairgowrie for Friday and Saturday night.  On Saturday we got to go and investigate rock pools, something Seth loves to do but we haven't been able to in a long time.  He also loved showing Holly the shells and Sea Stars he saw.  Very good friends Aaron and Kerry got married at Sorrento back beach a few weeks ago.  Unfortunately he wasn't able to go but was very impressed when he saw where they were married and recognised the beach from some of the photo's he's seen.  We also had one of Seth's best school mates James and his Mum, Dad and Sister come down Saturday night.  The four kids learned what slumber parties are all about and absolutely had a ball together.  Some may go and ask them to "SSSHHH, go to sleep", I loved hearing the giggles coming down the hallway.  Eventually they all crashed and it wasn't too late.  Sunday we headed to Mornington Racecourse for an "Easter Hunt".  We all enjoyed each other's company and had fun; all kids fell asleep on the way home.

This week Seth has been to school.  I love asking him what he did each day and getting responses like "I can't remember" and "played in the playground at lunchtime" and my absolute fave of all time "Dad!!! You're not that old yet, don't you remember what you did when you went to school, why do you always ask me that question?".  So school holidays are here again and this time Seth is well enough to do kid stuff and find out what holidays are all about instead of being in hospital and wondering how long until the next visitor comes.  First day of term 2 he has treatment at hospital, but day 2 looks like he'll be there!

Everyone have a great Easter and if you don't celebrate Easter, have a great break!

If you're not smiling, why not because Seth is,

Simon, Nikki, Seth and Holly

33

## Chapter 12

**10/04/13**

Hi

Seth is doing really well the last few weeks. He's enjoyed school holidays so far. We all had a super Easter; we also went to Etihad Stadium on Good Friday. Seth was filmed by Channel 7 with Batman but we don't know if he went to air. Seth had a blood test last Tuesday and all his results came back as rising which is great. We went to Blairgowrie for 6 nights. LOTS of beach, lots of rock pool investigating, lots of relaxing and Holly turned 2 so we celebrated it with brilliant sunny weather down there. We also went to Arthurs Seat to the Enchanted Maze, I still love that place.......it's so much fun. Now we're back home Seth has developed a mild case of Laryngitis along with a virus. That has slowed down his holiday plans BUT keep your fingers crossed it doesn't develop into anything more nasty so he can stay out of hospital. Monday he needs to go to the Monash for Chemo via his port and the dreaded Prednisilone (steroid) starts for another week, he is still having chemo everyday at home too. We have also seen a few cuts and bruises, it's hard not to jump up and down with raging excitement when he hurts himself. This week is 11 months since diagnosis, so it's been 11 months since he's been able to be a boy and run and play and jump etc. without having something restricting him so that's why it's hard not to get excited when he needs ice on his hand because he's jammed it on a swing. Next week school starts again and he can't wait for show and tell because of our trip to the beach, it's also the first trip anywhere since pre diagnosis.

So, if you're not smiling, why not because Seth is.

Have a great rest of the week,

Simon, Nikki, Seth and Holly.

P.S. He also had his sidies and back of his neck trimmed at Andrews Barbershop........His hair is growing back now because he doesn't have the type of Chemo that kills hair cells :)

*This is more things we do together that aren't inside, that aren't in outdoor areas that are high risk that I wrote about a few chapters ago. Once you put your mind to it, there really is no reason to stay inside or more to the point, do activities that are inside. The only issue with outside is of course the weather.*

**24/04/13**

Hi,

Seth's Laryngitis and virus have gone!!!! He missed the first week of school and Nikki had her hands full when I was at work with Seth on steroids and Holly trying to have fun with her brother. He ventured off last Monday to the Monash for his chemo and Friday night he started back on his oral chemo here at home. This week he is back at school and is also "Star of the week". This means he has a photo board in his class and each day he does something to help the kids learn about him. Today I wrote a letter which his teacher Mrs Bitoin told the class is a "special delivery" letter :) He is missing cricket and will be very pleased that Peter Siddle is named because he met him a few months ago at a kids clinic organised by Cricket Australia and his (our) mate Aaron at CA told me Peter would be there. He will also be disappointed that Bobby Quiney wasn't named.....it was hard explaining why his other cricket friends Clive Rose, Michael Hill and Jayde Herrick aren't on the team but he decided it's better for them not to be because they have more time to practise for next season. He's hoping to get to the under 12's footy training next Tuesday night and then their game the following Sunday. The coach is also a member of the cricket club and has asked Seth to help him coach a game or two.............He's not happy with himself for missing training with Duff and the boys last night because he took too long to do his homework.

On that note, if I didn't mention it last time, Holly turned 2 on the 8th of April and had a fantastic afternoon teas party down at Blairgowrie and this morning was her first time back to Playgroup so took along Freddo Frogs to have with the other kids.

Happy ANZAC day and remember,

If you're not smiling, why not because Seth is!

Simon, Nikki, Seth and Holly


*We were now well and truly into living with Leukaemia. We had a bag semi packed and things we used daily were easily accessible to throw into the bag. We had a few packets of band aids, some in the house and some in the car. We had plenty of batteries for the thermometer and fake candles Seth uses as a night light. We were given a letter from his Oncologists that explains his treatment and protocol that was for use whenever we went to the E.D. I'm sure some people waiting a long time and saw us walk in as soon as we got there wanted to know why. Again, a very high risk for infection, so Oncology patients need to be isolated to lessen the risk. By now we knew exactly what infection meant... Off to the hospital, E.D. if it was after hours and almost always a 5 day stay while Seth was on a I.V. antibiotic and being closely monitored with a blood test at 6am every morning. Remember a few chapters ago I mentioned his "port" the blood came from their too while he was on the ward so frequently he'd sleep through it. Also, food! No reheated food, no processed food unless his immunity was high. Processed as in salami etc. Ham needs to be no more than 2 days off the bone and the local supermarket got to know me by site and even if the deli had closed and the slicer was clean and packed away, they'd get whatever was needed. I liken it and think we were told to treat him as if he was pregnant with what food he was given, that way it would lessen the risk of infection... Don't worry, I got very used to hearing "risk of infection".*

## Chapter 13

**4/05/13**

Hi,

Seth has been juggling school and homework and blood tests and chemo and guess what?!?! He's still smiling!

He went to watch the Milo Cricket version of Soccer last week and decided it was for him. Today they drove up to Fox Rd Berwick and he said he didn't want to join in or play. Luckily pre-season training for cricket starts soon so he can go and watch some familiar faces which is why I think he doesn't want to participate in the Soccer programme.

We're also looking into non contact Kung Fu to try and teach him how to control little out bursts especially when he's on steroids which is every 4-6 weeks from memory.

He had another blood test yesterday and his Neutrophil's are 0.74. The game of finding a balance with his chemo dosages continues and he won't go to school next week to lessen the possibility of infection and of course risk. No transfusions are required which is fantastic news!!! He is also 2 weeks from finishing this treatment plan which means another operation to give him chemo via Lumbar Puncture.

Fast approaching is the 13th of May that will be one year since the trip to our GP and ultimately Monash ED and later confirmation of ALL T-Cell. What a year it has been!!! He has reinforced friendships, formed new friendships and had some amazing once in a lifetime opportunities. The most important is his new love of cricket, especially batting. I still strongly believe that all the people at Cricket Vic, Cricket Aus and the Narre South Cricket Club helped him cope with his illness and also he'd been admitted into hospital for a week approximately once a week with infection until he got involved with cricket and was only admitted for a week once and was going through some of the hardest body blowing chemo treatment at the time.

Holly has been by his side to the point that she will not go anywhere unless she can see him. Makes it very easy in shops to watch them both but I don't think it'll last. Every now and then Seth will move and when she realises there's a 2 year old voice calling "Sethy, Sethy, where's Sethy" then she finds him and the same voice calls out "There you are Sethy, you're not lost".

So, this week is a week of trying to not bring home infection for Nikki (she's back into dancing) and I so he doesn't get sick and then another blood test Friday.

Have a great weekend!!!

If you're not smiling, why not because Seth is!

Simon, Nikki, Seth and Holly


**13/05/13**

Hi,

Today is the 13/05. The first anniversary for Seth being taken to the Monash E.D.

By 11am we were told his blood wasn't clotting and to stay at home and watch for bruising (after a blood test with our G.P.). By 7.30pm he was at the E.D. starting to be poked and prodded. Seth Nikki and my Mum spent the night in the E.D. while tests were done to confirm their thoughts of Leukaemia. Before 10am on the 14th he was being wheeled into the Children's Cancer Centre with smiles on his face wondering how long the rash on his upper body was going to take to go away.........it was bruising as his platelets were so low his blood couldn't clot.

So, today one year on he has been to school, Holly went dancing, Nikki organised them and off to work I went.

Seth, Nikki, Holly and I have had friendships re-born, reinforced, new ones created and had an amazing journey with the Narre South Cricket Club, Cricket Australia and Cricket Victoria. From tears to laughter with your help, THANKYOU there is no way we could've got through the last year without you in our lives. Your e-mails, messages and phone calls mean to us than I suspect you realise.

If you're not smiling, why not because Seth is!
Simon, Nikki, Seth and Holly

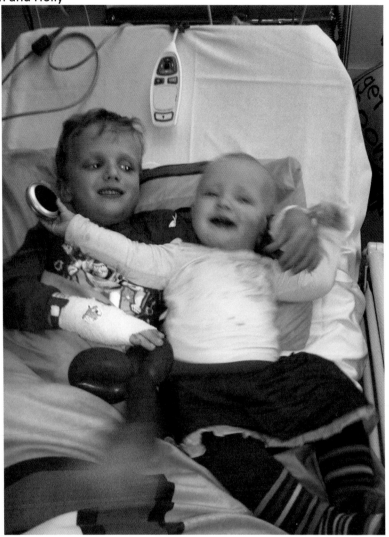

**24/05/13**

Hi
We made it through the five days of steroids with very few tantrums and minimal weight gain.
Last weekend Nikki went away Saturday night on a Mums retreat and Seth, Holly and I made it through the weekend without any starvation or broken bones.
This week Seth has been back at school and tried Kung Fu Wednesday night.  We will go back this Wednesday to leave him there as he wouldn't participate much with us around, but enjoyed it when he did.  Holly tried Callisthenics and loved it.  This weekend is a trip to St Kilda tomorrow and then Auskick Sunday morning and off to Aaron and Kerry's Sunday afternoon to say hi and have a play with Maggie and meet Indi (dogs).  Thursday is the revised day for Seth to drive a steam train on Puffing Billy, watch out John Seth's getting excited!
Have a great weekend.
Remember, if you're not smiling why not because Seth is,
Simon, Nikki, Seth and Holly

**26/05/13**

Hi,

As promised here is a pic of Seth and his hair!!!

It was taken today with his fave footy player Dale Thomas as well as Alan Didak and Alan Toovey. They were down at Bayside Chrysler, Jeep, Dodge and Nissan in Frankston today. They are three of the nicest blokes, they included Holly as well as Seth and Didak gave Seth some tips in the showroom. No damage but an Alfa got a footy in its bumper a few times. All from a Dad at School that works there and knows Seth loves the Pies, Stuart again thanks.

Thomas reminds me a little of Michael Hill and Jayde Herrick from the Victorian Bushrangers (Cricket), no matter how many times he hunted him down, whatever was being done was stopped and 100% attention was given to Seth.

Have a great week,

If you're not smiling, why not?

Simon, Nikki, Seth and Holly.

*This day was organised by a friend that worked at the car dealership. It was a promotion, but I was told later that Seth was the highlight of the day. I spoke to all three players and I always had an invincible type thought about the players on the ground. I quickly learned how wrong I was when one of them said "I knew Seth was coming, I didn't know he'd have hair. He has opened my eyes to more than what I see when I visit the RCH (Melbourne). How do you as a parent wake every morning and not know if you'll get through the day without needing to go to the hospital?" As a parent Nikki & I couldn't think about whether we'd need to go to the hospital, we had a routine in the morning of a quick look at Seth (without him realising) and asking a few questions. He then said "I will be a better person able to offer more when I visit the ward after meeting you Simon, Seth is amazing and Holly is such a beautiful little sister."*

**30/05/13**

Hi,

WHAT A WEEK!!!!

Friday will mark the end of 3 continuous weeks at school for Seth (except for student free days and chemo one day)!

Saturday we went to St Kilda and then on our way home stopped at The Block Skyhigh. Not much activity but they are still going.

Seth got a participation award at Auskick and can't wait to get his free large pizza. After Auskick we took off down to Frankston and met Alan Toovey, Alan Didak and Seth's FAVE Dale Thomas all from the Collingwood Football Club. They signed a footy, his club jumper and a piece of paper for the cricket club coach, Mick. Didak gave Seth some tips and they played in the showroom of the car dealer we were at. Every now and then Seth would disappear out of sight and Holly and I would find him talking to Thomas. Holly and Seth had their faces painted, jumped on the jumping castle, hunted the players down and said good bye and we were off, back to Berwick to catch up with Aaron and Kerry. Both Seth and Holly wore out Maggie, Indi and Kerry's parent's dog Tilley.....ssshhhh I think Az may have been a little tired too.

This week Holly went dancing, Seth went back to Kung Fu (and loves it) and today he got to drive a steam train on Puffing Billy Railway. We went to Belgrave and Fleur gave us a quick tour of the workshop (we were a little late) and then off to the carriage we went. We were in a full carriage for about 20 minutes and then it was ours. When we got to Lakeside Seth and I jumped up into the driver's cabin and Kevin the driver was brilliant, Seth released the brake and off we went. Once the engine was coupled back up to carriages we went back to talk to the Station Master, Conductor etc and fed the wild birds.

Hopefully next week will slow down a little in preparation for the week after when Seth will have chemo daily at hospital.

If you're not smiling why not because Seth is,

Simon, Nikki, Seth and Holly.

## Chapter 14

**10/06/13**

Hi,

It's been a great few weeks. Seth has done really well with not picking up a cold at school or anywhere else. He's been able to go to a few parties and visit the supermarket and shopping centre. This weekend we spent a night away and we are all a little revived now. Seth had a blood test yesterday morning and we were hoping to watch Collingwood train, unfortunately pathology in the hospital was busy so we didn't get there so we head to Blairgowrie from there. Tomorrow Seth will start 5 days of daily visits to hospital for chemo via his port. He also got a hair neaten up last Saturday afternoon. He nearly has enough hair for a full haircut but has told us he wants to grow it longer.

So I am keeping this one short and sweet, have a great week.

If you're not smiling why not because Seth is

Simon, Nikki, Seth and Holly


**11/06/13**

Hi,

Why do I always sign off "If you're not smiling why not because Seth is"?

This pic (taken today) is of Seth hooked up to his daily chemo treatment that is until Saturday.

A picture says a thousand words, I think there's more in this one.

Simon, Nikki, Seth and Holly

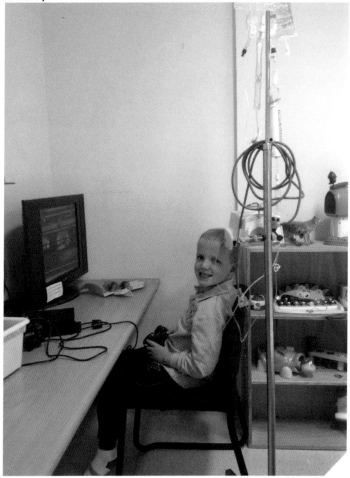

**25/06/13**

Hi all

Keep the messages coming back, Seth loves reading them....yes he reads them!!! Not bad for only basically completing term 1 of prep last year and missing 36 days (7+ weeks) of grade one so far this year. Just shows how much the school helps Seth and Nikki with information to keep him up to date and then of course the extra work when he goes to school.

He has had a cold since last Monday night and still soldiers on. Holly has it a little and Nikki got it late last week. This morning he had a blood test to check what's happening and whether his chemo needs to be adjusted and then off to school. By the time you read this Nikki would've picked him up again as it's a half day.

We also got the news that his "wish" with Starlight Foundation has been granted so he'll get a new cubby with a slide, climbing wall, climbing net etc. near the end of July. Then a few people have volunteered to help get it built for him and once it's up he'll have a ribbon cutting ceremony also organised with Starlight Foundation.

It's nearly the end of term 2 and we will be doing some things that we haven't been able to do until now, including lunch with staff from Cricket Victoria at the MCG cafe. Hopefully he'll be ok because he has a visit to the hospital for chemo the Monday before and it is also a dreaded steroid week.

SOOOO................... If you're not smiling why not because Seth is,

Simon, Nikki, Seth and Holly

P.S. Let's hope it's not running at 12.07pm Sunday because I'm running 300m down Southbank in only fluoro board shorts to raise money for the Leukaemia Foundation (I might also be in the local papers because I have been asked to do a few media interviews).

**15/07/13**

Hi,

What a sensational school holidays Seth and Holly have had!!!

This week is a steroid week and the trick with steroids is to keep Seth active.......as you will read below, Nikki has done a great job with the help of some very special friends to do exactly that.

This is the first school holidays since diagnosis that Seth has been able to do anything. All the others he's either been in hospital fighting infection or at home too sick to leave the house.

This week alone, has been amazing and just when you watch him and think WOW that smile is so big, it gets bigger. Monday he had chemo at Monash in Clayton, it was the first time his Poppy has been in Melbourne and been able to go with Seth to the Children's Cancer Centre. Poppy has been with Seth to the E.D. and to the ward, now he has a full understanding of what Seth goes through BUT also what wonderful things are available to help pass time while he is in the Children's Cancer Centre.

Tuesday Seth, Holly and Nikki went to the Docklands to see the circus which Challenge - supporting kids with cancer gave those tickets and also the carnival. They were amazed and stuck to their seats during the show apparently and then later they were lucky enough to have photo's taken and Nikki was talking to the person with the photographer that was the owner and gave Seth and Holly coupons to go on rides as well.

Wednesday we had the pleasure of having lunch with Rohan and Chris from Cricket Victoria and Aaron from Cricket Australia (Seth is hoping next time Lauren can see him, Lauren took him under her wing when he was 13th man for the Vic Bushrangers last year), at none other than a cafe at the "G". Before lunch we had a tour of Cricket Victoria's office and met lots of staff, (still lots to meet though) amazing people down there - "Ship" the coach remembered Seth among many others. It was fantastic to see where they work, but also the trophies and Seth was very impressed by the Cricket Cards on the display on one of the walls, (I think they are from the 1980's) as he is collecting Football Cards. After lunch we went over to Cricket Australia's office and met a few more people including James Sutherland to which I am very embarrassed as I didn't make the connection at the time for James role of running C.A. Then we went back to the G and were taken to the Sports Museum. Bailey and Aaron gave up their lunch break to spend time with Seth and he loved everything down there, mostly the 3D Shane Warne "show" but he also liked the 3D James Hird "show" too. He couldn't believe how many different types and shapes of cricket bats too. Then we left there and Aaron took us down into the bellows of the G to the training nets. We watched an indigenous training session for a little while and left. I think Seth dreamt about cricket that night and I can't thank everyone enough for a brilliant day and being made to feel so welcome!

Thursday Seth watch "Epic" with his Nonna and he didn't like it. He said it was scary. Then Seth, Holly and Nikki went to Dandenong Stadium and met D.Q. and Tony from the Rangers basketball team and they played basketball for an hour and a half. Dribbling, shooting and both Seth and Holly even did their first slam dunk! A big thanks to Daniel for arranging the meet and play!

Today is Mummy and kid morning and then off to one of Seth's mate's house this afternoon for a play and a well earned glass of wine for Nikki :)

Well, next week he will be back at school and fingers crossed, doesn't go back to hospital for two weeks which is when his next lumber puncture is due.

If you're not smiling why not because Seth is,

Simon, Nikki, Seth and Holly

**31/07/13**

Hi,

Seth is back at school and LOVING it!!

He had a fantastic school holidays and loved telling everyone at school about what he did. He's also excited because Kung Fu has started back and he loves the socialisation of different aged kids and don't tell him I told you, but he has already developed a respect for Master Richard. I also think Master Richard has a respect him as he can see Seth is committed (at the moment). Through a mate (Dave - World Wide Martial Arts Wholesalers) I was asked to contact Sensei Bruce Haynes. Sensei is from a Karate background but believes martial arts is a family. Seth was invited to meet him and some other martial arts specialist last weekend at an event. Seth, Holly and Nikki went and Seth came back so positive and so inspired to continue his Kung Fu. He also met Rob Gear (Hanshi Khan 10th Degree Black Belt). Rob came down from Sydney and heard about Seth before he arrived. Rob took Seth aside and had a chat, gave him some pointers and also a hoodie and t-shirt. The hoodie is to keep Seth warm because Rob is fighting adult Leukaemia and he gets cold when he is getting his chemo. Bruce, Rob and everyone else Seth, Holly and Nikki met, a BIG thanks!!!

Unfortunately I couldn't go because I was helping Mick get the Agi pipe in our backyard and trying to get the ground levels ready for Seth's cubby that is his wish that has been granted by Starlight Foundation. After any times getting the machine bogged and the last time nearly needing to get a car to tow it out, Mick (mainly) and I dug the trenches by hand and laid the Agi. The levels will be done later when the yard dries out.....may even be after the cubby goes up at this stage with Melbourne's rain.

This week Seth is being Seth and going to school, Kung Fu and doing homework. Next week he will have chemo via lumbar puncture at hospital.

If you're not smiling why not because Seth is,

Simon, Nikki, Seth and Holly.

43

## Chapter 16

**07/08/13**

Hi,

Seth has had his Lumbar Puncture. He was very hungry when he woke so he's had lunch....sandwich, chocolate cup cake, fruit, juice and some sort of lolly I think. He's about to leave the hospital and trek down Wellington Rd (for the hhmmmm lost count of the amount of times) to come home. It's a steroid week so by the weekend he'll be bouncing of poor Holly, the walls and whatever else gets in his way so I think a trip to the cricket nets a few times will be in order and also Auskick on Sunday.
If you're not smiling why not because Seth is
Simon, Nikki, Seth and Holly

**21/08/13**

Hi,

Seth has been enjoying going to school and going up a few levels in reading. Thursday we went to Collingwood Football Club training and got some autographs and photos with some of the players. Seth was very impressed to meet the coach - Nathan Buckley, but was a little disappointed Dale Thomas and Alan Didak weren't there. I saw Harry O'Brien but unfortunately didn't get the opportunity to talk to him, I find him to be fascinating and would love to have a chat one day, Challenge - Supporting Kids with Cancer organised the morning. Seth also liked having lunch at the Westpac Centre - Collingwood Football Club Headquarters. Then we wondered off to see Seth's fave, Lauren at Cricket Victoria because when we were last there she was on holidays. We were also lucky enough to have a chat with Rohan, Annie, Michael and Aaron while we were there and Seth didn't seem to mind that we didn't see any cricketers. Last weekend we went to Sydney for a Baptism and managed to find time to spend Saturday afternoon at Tooronga Zoo. We caught a ferry over and Seth and Holly were both very excited to see the Opera House, Harbour Bridge and Navy boats. We weren't able to see the whole Zoo but next time we go, we will be there for more than a few days so we can see the whole Zoo and catch up with friends and family. It was also Holly's first ride in a plane and she loved it! A BIG thanks to Liz, Andy and Izzy for their hospitality and driving us around. Seth and Holly both ask about Izzy constantly. Today Seth's new cubby arrived that has been donated to him by Starlight Foundation, they also surprised him (and us) with some extra toys, a new table and chairs for inside the cubby and a table tennis table which Seth can't wait for it to be together so he can beat me again! The consignment note said it weighs 1000kg!!!! I also don't have the time to count how many pieces of timber is there, but our garage floor is full. This Saturday a few people are coming over to try our best to get it up in one day......keep your fingers crossed because I need to disappear for 2 hours for cricket club stuff and I'm not sure if we'll have enough hands so if you have a spare hour or day let me know.....We start at 7am Saturday, even if it's to man the BBQ for lunch, we also need 2 in the garage sorting out the pieces into sections.
Seth made it through another week of steroids two weeks ago and will have a week of hospital visits in about three weeks........OH I nearly forgot!!! On Monday Seth went to his first physio appointment and we were told his glutes, abs and somewhere else had depleted due to chemo and he was shown some strengthening exercises to do until he starts one day a week for six weeks to try and strengthen them again. Nikki then took him to the Children's Cancer Centre because he has a cough and we wanted to check it out, even though he was still being himself in terms of energy etc. He has Viral Pneumonia!! His coughing is breaking the build up in his lungs down so there's no need to x-ray, admit to hospital etc. We just need to monitor him but, next time I get a sniffle I don't think I'll be anything but embarrassed if I complain after watching Super Seth not complain at all.
If you're not smiling, why not, because Seth is
Simon, Nikki, Seth and Holly

**10/09/13**

Hi,

Here's a pic of Seth's cubby.

It will be painted over the next few weeks.

A big thanks to all that helped! It was a big job but everyone that worked on it agreed that once Seth got on it and his smile was seen... it was all well worth it!!!!

If you're not smiling why not because Seth is

Simon, Nikki, Seth and Holly

**10/09/13**

Hi,

Seth has had a hard few weeks and come out the other side with smiles. He had daily visits to Monash for chemo last week and now he won't have that particular chemo again which is fantastic! It also means that we are about 6 weeks from the end of cycle 3 of 3 for this stage of treatment AND that will also be approximately 2 years of chemo left.

He has physio to help his muscles and of course Kung Fu. Saturday we went to Malvern with 14 friends (Sorry to those not invited, he had to cut down from over 50 friends he wanted to take) to a place called The Art Factory in Malvern and they all had a ball celebrating his wish from Starlight Foundation being granted. His cubby (Starlight Foundation wish) was also finished Saturday and is now ready for playing on and painting.

A **MASSIVE** thank you to Dylan, Pete, Mick, Alan, Mustaffa, Bill, Gary and Dylan (yes we had 2 Dylan's) for all your hard work! Nikki, Seth, Holly and I can't say thank you enough for your tireless work and also some of you returning from start to finish and giving up 3 Saturdays. It didn't seem to matter whether you came from next door, Pakenham or Ballarat for that matter, you just did it for

Seth with smiles. I have called Seth's Cubby Photo Album - "Seth's new cubby - Donated by Starlight Foundation, Built by mates who love Seth".

He was also invited to a birthday party and he went on a Go Kart and played laser tag for the first time. He got off the kart all sweaty, thirsty and needing ventolin ............... a little early to say but it looks like he's got my gene that enjoys driving fast and competitively.

This Sunday we are going to watch the Dandenong Rangers senior men's team play in the Grand Final and will probably be when we say goodbye to Daequon, Jamie and Keyana Montreal and Tony Lewis. DQ and Tony had a great season but it's time for them to go home to the U.S. Maybe they'll get another contract and be back next season????

If you're not smiling, why not, because Seth is

Simon, Nikki, Seth and Holly

P.S. Saturday night we went to the MCG to see Collingwood lose to Port Adelaide, it was Seth's 2nd and Holly and Nikki's 1st live AFL game. A BIG thanks to Challenge - Supporting Kids With Cancer for the tickets, we had a great time!!!!

## 24/09/13

This email went only to Starlight Foundation:

Hi,

I will get some pics sent later tonight or early tomorrow BUT I'm too excited and amazed at Seth to wait!!!!!!!!!!!!!!!!!!!!!!!!!!!!!!!!!!!!!!!!!!!!!!!

Seth saw an ad on TV about Starlight movie month and told his mum he wanted to do it (last week). He also said that he'd give his $5 from the Tooth Fairy he got a few weeks ago from his first ever tooth!!!!! So he and Nikki set about looking at what is needed to organise it.

They decided on tonight at 5pm. Since starting on the weekend with inviting people, it has grown so has been changed to 4pm. It was also a PJ movie night, now it's a PJ disco and movie night.

Seth has a Starlight donation page now set up, the local Coles is donating popcorn and lollies, the local Lombards has donated streamers, decorations and balloons and we are waiting for the local pizza shop to open to see if they'll help out.

We sat down with Seth and decided our goal was $75, but to reach $100 would be brilliant.

He has already reached $100 on his page and there is still a fair few kids coming that haven't donated :)

When I asked him why he wants to do it, he replied with "I want to have fun in my school holidays because I am normally in hospital and they gave me my cubby. If I get some money from my friends to give to them, other kids might be able to get a cubby too"

Proud is what I am, so proud of Seth!!!!!!

Anyway, I'll send some pics soon,

If you're not smiling, why not, because Seth is.

Simon

## 25/09/13

Hi,

It's been interesting in the Sleep household the last few weeks.

We went and watched the Dandenong Rangers Men's basketball team win the SEABL championship. Seth's friends from the U.S., Tony and DQ played really well. DQ was awarded MVP. They haven't confirmed as they only just got back to the U.S. and their families earlier this week, but the Dandenong Rangers website has announced they both re-signed for next season... Seth can hardly wait the 5 months until they're back.

46

Holly got a terrible bug that lasted a week, luckily it was contained to only her.  I got a migraine, luckily I got the medication quick enough and it was a dull roar after the first 12 hours.

Seth has decided that he'd like to do some fundraising for all the charities that have helped him.  So as his first, he picked Starlight Foundation - Movie Night.  Last week he saw an ad for it and asked Nikki if he could do it.  They sat down and wrote down a list of names and a list of what's needed.  Last night kicked off at 4pm and it was a "Pyjama Disco and Movie Night".  He was hoping to raise $75 and said it would be really good if he got $100.  He raised $330.

School holidays are here and he isn't in hospital!!!!!!  Seth, Holly and Nikki and checking the internet each day and picking something to do.  He still has physio once a week, chemo tablets each day and others like antibiotics every second day etc.  Monday he will be back to Monash for a day visit and the dreaded steroids will also start for that week.

He is disappointed that the Magpies didn't make it to the Grand Final but is happy with Hawks and Freo.

If you're not smiling why not because Seth is

Simon, Nikki, Seth and Holly

**10/10/13**

Hi,

The school holidays have come and gone and Seth enjoyed nearly all of them. Last week he had 5 days of steroids and this time only ate half the house, I eat a lot and he was out eating me at the dinner table some nights. The combination of steroids and his chemo tablet being lifted from 75% (last 9 months or so) to 100% has knocked him around a little. He can't sleep before midnight and is up and still tired at 6.30am. We suspect that a combination of last week's steroids, his chemo and other medication being raised has all been the cause of no sleep, fingers crossed it settles down and he can get back to normal.

He loved being able to do normal kid things while on holidays with his friends and of course his sister Holly. They did art and craft, 10 pin bowling, playing at the park, catching up with friends, saw a few movies with his Nonna and Mum and has started to plan his Christmas holiday activities already. Although he didn't feel well last weekend, we went to see Silvers Circus at Southland on Sunday and we all loved the show!!! We were also introduced to the owner of the circus. Anna is such a wonderful lady and spoilt Seth and Holly rotten!!!! She gave them a show bag each, ice cream, fairy floss, Seth even got a light up sword and clown teddy. On the way home we weren't sure what his body was going to do to him, but after a rest in the car and some more food and drink he perked back up. Monday he went back to school for the morning and then back to Monash for more physio and another podiatry appointment. Both Dr's said he's improving and doing really well! Just before he was taken to the E.D. May last year he learnt to ride without training wheels. He couldn't ride his bike until a few months or so ago so he asked for his training wheels to go back on (Dad was pleased because if his platelets are a little low, a scratch of bruise will take a long time to heal if he fell off), well a minor break through during the holidays!!! He asked for one training wheel to come off and the other be lifted so he can try and ride on 2 wheels :)

Holly loved Seth being home and on Monday was asking where Seth was frequently because she wanted her big brother to play with her. She is still enjoying dancing and her first ever concert is fast approaching. She is also trying really hard to be big like her brother and give up the nappies, so far she's got a pretty good strike/miss rate but she only started yesterday afternoon and Nikki and I are still amazed after us asking her for so long to do it, that she just walked up and told Nikki that's what she wants to do.

If you're not smiling, why not, because Seth is!

Simon, Nikki, Seth and Holly

**17/10/13**

Hi,

Seth has had a hard few weeks and come out the other side with smiles. He had daily visits to Monash for chemo and now he won't have that particular chemo again which is fantastic! It also means that we are about 6 weeks from the end of cycle 3 of 3 for this stage of treatment.

He has physio to help his muscles and of course Kung Fu. Yesterday we went to Malvern with 14 friends to a place called The Art Factory and they all had a ball celebrating his wish from Starlight

Foundation being granted.  His cubby was also finished yesterday and is now ready for playing on and painting.

I will update you all with more detail soon.

If you're not smiling, why not, because Seth is

Simon, Nikki, Seth and Holly

P.S. Last night we went to the MCG to see Collingwood lose to Port Adelaide, it was Seth's 2nd and Holly and Nikki's 1st live AFL game.  BIG thanks to Challenge - Supporting Kids with Cancer for the tickets, we had a great time!!!!

## Chapter 18

**4/11/13**

Hi,

A very quick update!!!

Seth finished his 5 days of steroid this morning and now we are in our 18th month of treatment, Nikki has finetuned how to keep Seth from going crazy while taking it. Today he went and saw his friend Andrew from Andrews Barbershop in Beaconsfield and had his first full haircut since about July last year as chemo took it away in August.

One thing I notice in this pic is that he is definitely growing up and growing up fast!!!

If you're not smiling, why not, because Seth is

Simon, Nikki, Seth and Holly


**10/11/13**

Hi,

As you know, Seth had his first haircut last week, since mid last year. He has been at school every day this term and loving it! Not only is he more self confident after his haircut but he has also gone up another level with his reading. He is already talking about who he hopes is in his class, who his teacher is and which room he'll be in for next year. We have not been told yet, but I think he has missed about 50 school days so far this year... MUCH better than 3 terms last year. Although, he still has 5 or so weeks of school left and will need a few days off for chemo during this time. Seth, Holly and Nikki were part of the Santa Parade at Fountain Gate (Westfield) on Saturday morning. Unfortunately he wouldn't wear his entire "Puss in Boots" costume but they enjoyed the walk. The physio he had until a few weeks ago has definitely helped his leg muscles because he walked the whole 45 minutes. He started back at Milo In2 Cricket this weekend and loves it. He managed to participate for 1 hour and 25 minutes of the 1 hour and 30 minute session and although he was tired, still found enough energy to go to a mate from school's birthday party afterwards. He will have another blood test on Wednesday and although we can't see symptoms that he needs another platelet or full blood ETC. transfusion, it will confirm. It will also tell his Dr's whether he needs to have his chemo dosage adjusted.

If you're not smiling, why not, because Seth is

Simon, Nikki, Seth and Holly

**14/11/13**

Hi,

I know, I sent an update out the other day BUT how quickly things can change when fighting Leukaemia.

Seth had a blood test on Wednesday (yesterday) which was "routine" and then off to school. His Neutrophil's are 0.15, they need to be over 1.0 to not be Neutropenic. This means he stops chemo and has a higher than normal risk of getting an infection and if he does, he will be needing IV antibiotics. If this was to be needed, he would be admitted into hospital because he is so low. The bonus is that the other parts of his blood, like platelets are still high enough to not need to consider another transfusion. So, he is staying home from school at the moment and although he is missing his mates, his teacher Mrs Bitoin is making sure he has plenty to do while he's at home so he won't fall too far behind. Tuesday he'll have another blood test, depending on those results, he will start chemo again and be back at school on Wednesday ....... keep your fingers crossed and pray his body can do it so quickly.

On another note, Nikki and Holly's dancing concert is getting closer and even in all the Christmas lead up and dress rehearsals in Warragul and practising after work, during the week, one of the ladies Nikki dances with gave Seth a Christmas CD, Jay Laga'aia's latest one and Holly a new Wiggles CD. Seth has been listening to it since he got it Tuesday and loves it, he loves Jay. It helped him relax and be able to get to sleep a little easier and I decided last night to try and send Jay an e-mail thanking him. Well, I did send a quick e-mail to him and I expected a PR person to read it and reply. Jay read it and Jay replied. He didn't reply in the usual return e-mail though, he didn't put fingers to keyboard; he posted a message on Facebook. It is attached and may take a little while to load due to it being a big file, but well worth the wait, even if you only watch into the first few bars BUT it is

51

worth watching it to the end.

Amazing that such a busy person, that himself is working away from his family, takes time to do this for someone that he has never met and it wasn't because someone that works with him told him to or because someone pulled some strings, he did it from his heart and for that THANKYOU Jay Laga'aia!!

If you're not smiling, why not, because Seth is

Simon, Nikki, Seth and Holly


**20/11/13**

Hi,

Seth has been admitted to hospital because he was a couple of days at or just under 38 degrees and his Neutrophil's are at 0.05, so nearly nonexistent. He is happy and has had an x-ray, more blood tests and is having IV antibiotics. We are hoping the test come back as viral and his neutrophil lift so he can come home by the weekend. I will update more tomorrow night.

If you're not smiling, why not, because Seth is

Simon, Nikki, Seth and Holly


**21/11/13**

Hi,

I am back home tonight with Holly after spending the night with Seth in hospital.

Tuesday he had a blood test and his Neutrophil's were 0.05, his temp was high 37 degrees. Tuesday night he went to the E.D. at about 10pm and was admitted to the ward somewhere after 2am. Wednesday his Neutrophil's were 0.01, so they were dropping and the best place to be was in hospital. Today his Neutrophil's are 0.02, FANTASTIC.... they're improving. Since going to the E.D. he's had his port accessed which is a little valve under his ribs that has a line going under his ribs and into a vein in his neck. Through the port is saline for hydration and every 6 hours is an antibiotic. Once a day he was having another antibiotic, he had that this morning at 1am ...... as he's hooked up, he sleeps through it. He has a blood test each day and this morning that was by a finger prick which he doesn't like because his port wouldn't let any out. He also had a nasal swab, urine sample and x-ray yesterday. Thorough? I think they are!

I'll try to break down why it was all done -

One of the first signs of infection is a rise in body temperature, if he gets to 38 we need to contact the hospital, start monitoring at time intervals the Docs specify and potentially go to hospital. Due to his immunity being low, we have a letter from the Children's Cancer Centre that gets him straight through triage and into the E.D. because he is at a very high risk of further infection if he sits in the E.D. with everyone else.

The blood tests tell the Dr's what his body is doing, it shows Neutrophil's which is his immunity, it shows his platelet level which is what clots blood, it shows his Haemoglobin and a lot of other things. If his levels are rising, he is able to come home.

As to Neutrophil's, if he was well, he'd be somewhere between 5.0 and 8.0 (from memory), he needs to be over 1.0 while on chemo but not over 2.0.

He is put on I.V. antibiotics before results are found as a precaution and of course, the sooner he is started, the sooner he can get better and also reduce the infection if that's what he has.

The nasal swab and urine sample is to test for an infection and then what type. It also is tested for viruses.

The x-ray is to check his chest for pneumonia because he has a cough and is also highly prone to it while fighting Leukaemia.

So, this morning the Oncology team came around and told Seth and I that they'd stop the once a day antibiotic. They also said that the x-ray was clear and all tests only returned a mild virus. They decided it was best for him to stay on the 6 hourly antibiotics for another 24 hours, which is why he is still there. If tomorrow's 6am blood test comes back at 10am with his Neutrophil's rising and he doesn't have a temperature, they'll most likely discharge him.... this is not guaranteed though. While I was with him, last night Nikki, Holly, Seth and I had dinner together and then Nikki and Holly came home. Seth and I then had a long chat and watched TV He fell asleep by 9pm and woke at 6am. Today we drew pictures, watched the two messages that Jay Laga'aia sent him recently via Facebook, watched TV, played board games, drew pictures, wrote stories, ate, drank and were generally having fun. This morning my mum came in and spent a few hours also drawing and helping Seth write stories. Twice today he had "Skype" with his class and also the Paediatric teacher spent some time with him. Although it seems like a lot, when sitting still and confined to one room, it is a long day and we did still go a little crazy. He had a visit from a mate called Dominic too. Dominic was there to have a blood test in the cancer centre and his mum, sister, Nan and himself came up to see him. Nikki and Holly got there about 4ish and we all had dinner, chats, read stories and Holly and I were in the car heading home at about 6.30 / 7 o'clock.

We are hoping that he can come home tomorrow (Friday) but we will find out in the morning. If he does come home, he'll still be going back on Monday to have chemo via his port on Monday. He will then most likely have a weekly blood test and when his Neutrophil's get back to 1.0, he'll start on oral chemo again.

If you're not smiling, why not, because Seth is

Simon, Nikki, Seth and Holly


**25/11/13**

Hi,

Holly had her first concert and decided Seth wasn't there, so she wasn't going to do it. Nikki was on stage happily dancing to the Wiggles, trying to get Holly to do it. Nikki had her concert and enjoyed it. She did four dances through the concert and I was told by Tahlia (our neighbour that went with her) that it was a great concert and Nikki did really well.

Seth spent the weekend at home and is doing his best not to go crazy. Yesterday he and I got on the tools and set up his new table tennis table, that has helped him pass time a lot, especially while it's raining and he can't go in the backyard to his cubby. Today we went back to Monash for his monthly IV chemo. Hi Neutrophil's are 0 that means he has no self made immunity. He is on antibiotics for longer, needs to stay isolated and will have another blood test on Friday. If the results aren't improving on Monday, he'll be back to the Monash on Monday and most likely be admitted again. He's only been able to go to one Milo In2 Cricket session this year, out of 4 and won't be able to go to the last one for the year this weekend. Let's hope he can go in January!! It also means he'll be off school for at least this week.  OH and this week is a steroid week, so being isolated and full of extra steroid induced energy is going to be very hard for him not to go mad!!!!!

This article is online;
http://www.cricketvictoria.com.au/news/article/the-road-to-recovery
It is one year since they did the article on Seth and wanted to do a follow up, AMAZING to care so much about Seth and wanting to keep others informed too.
If you're not smiling, why not, because Seth is
Simon, Nikki, Seth and Holly

**29/11/13**

Hi,
Here is the cubby ...... finished!!!!
Thank you so much and Seth is 0.06 Neutrophil's, so it will be used a lot while he can't go to school.
Thanks,
Simon, Nikki, Seth and Holly.
P.S. Stay tuned for loads of pics with loads of kids playing on it.
P.P.S. Jessie, please pass around the office so everyone can see what a 6 year old boy dreams about and what it looks like when his dream comes true.

**05/12/13**

54

Good morning,

We all survived another week of Seth being on steroids. His neutrophil was at 0.06 last week and so we spent the weekend at home. He and Holly really amaze me! We couldn't go to a Christmas party on Saturday or a birthday party on Sunday. Nikki and Holly went to their trophy presentation for dancing on Saturday night and they both just made the most of what they could and didn't worry about what they might be missing out on. Ian from Ideal Painting and his team came back and guess what....... Seth's cubby is finished!!!! He's very happy with his colour choice and now he wants to have his mates over for a ribbon cutting ceremony. He is happy to wait for Christmas to be over and everyone can settle down before he has it, I think there are so many wonderful people that helped build it and we'll need to do 2 or 3 ribbon cutting ceremonies. He also missed the last session of Milo Cricket for the year. Last year we thought he'd only get to 1 or 2 sessions, he went to nearly all of them. This year we thought he'd go to all of them, unfortunately he's only been well enough to go to 1 out of 4. My fingers are crossed he will say well and get to all Milo Cricket sessions next year. "Lights on Glasscocks" is a house near us that have an amazing light display every December. They allowed Seth to go through their display with Nikki alone and just like last year, offered to do it at anytime. Monday Seth had another blood test at Casey Hospital and then off to Monash for a review with his Dr. The little bugger!!!! His neutrophil lifted to 1.99!!!! Tuesday he went back to school and yesterday he went on an excursion to a swim school with his class. Last night he went back to Kung Fu and loved it. Nikki said that Holly "got in trouble" because she was showing the parents how big she is and that she can dance and then once that was enough, she started to show them that she was big enough to do Kung Fu and copied her brother. After the last "Seth catch up" e-mail, I got a request to tell everyone about my hobbies. I don't have a hobby at the moment, I don't have time between work and what Seth and Holly get up to. When I get time to start a hobby, I'll let you know. Also, as his immunity is back up, he can go and see Santa and have a photo taken... I hope Holly will too, she's happy with Santa at a safe distance or if he has a lolly for her, otherwise she will have nothing at all to do with him.

If you're not smiling, why not, because Seth is

Simon, Nikki, Seth and Holly


**10/12/13**

Hi,

Seth went back to school last Tuesday. Not only was he excited but almost the whole school. His class mates were very excited to see him, his teacher apparently couldn't stop smiling all day and he was the talk of the playground. It's nearly the end of another school year and although he was at school more than last year, the school support is amazing! This weekend we went to Anglesea. We stayed at the "Beachfront Caravan Park" and it was such a fantastic place. I can't recommend the park or staff enough, they really did go above and beyond to help and make us welcome. Why did we go there Friday night? Camp Quality took us and 12 other families, that's why. CQ run quite a few camps throughout the year and as their slogan says "Laughter is the best medicine". We also caught up with a few volunteers we met at the camp we went to at Phillip Island last year. Dave, Tamara and Nicky were there and although Holly didn't remember them, Seth did and that helped Holly settle in because her brother was relaxed. In fact they settled in so well, Saturday morning Nikki and I went with other parents to a cafe and had a coffee, cake and chat! When we got back we were looked at and then they continued to finish their artwork. Saturday night a guy named Valanga

55

who emigrated from the Republic of South Africa travelled all the way to Anglesea from Frankston to keep us all entertained with his jokes and stories whilst playing the drums, in fact teaching us all how to play.  Sunday was a beach carnival and as you can see by the pic, Seth was 1st to pick up the cricket bat, Holly actually was 2nd which was a surprise.  The Anglesea Lions Club and Anglesea Lionesses made sure we were fed.  BBQ, sandwiches, BBQ chicken, salads, cakes, hotdogs, cakes, sandwiches and more cakes.  I also had a chat to the president (my Dad is Ballarat Lions Club President) and he told me they helped last year and hope to keep helping in years to come.  Also, all the food we ate was donated by local businesses, what a wonderful community to get together and help people from out of town!  Also the Anglesea Cancer Council supplied the cakes.  Between the activities (even Bunnings set up a few things), the eating and the entertainment provided we all got home absolutely exhausted and yet so very relaxed.  Today Seth will have another blood test and the results will then depend on whether his oral chemo is changed.  On Sunday he's been invited to the Melbourne Stars Family Day at Casey Fields.  Melbourne Stars is a cricket team that play in the 20/20 Big Bash League.  Watch out for pics of that next week!  Last year he was spoilt with meeting Shane Warne and Sir Viv Richards along with catching up with some of the Vic players and meeting some others.  He can't wait to see Clive Rose again.  Clive was 12th man for Vic last season when Seth was the 13th man.

We also got to see Santa and have a photo..... you need to wait until closer to Christmas to see it, but Holly was not impressed AT ALL!!  A few weeks ago she thought Santa was Papa Smurf, after explaining the difference she will take a lolly off him, but that's about all.

If you're not smiling, why not, because Seth is

Simon, Nikki, Seth and Holly

**17/12/13**


**Merry Christmas and a Happy New Year** to each and every one of you!

A big thanks for your help and support through the year.

If you're not smiling, why not because Seth is

Simon, Nikki, Seth and Holly


**30/12/13**

Hi,

We hope you all had a great Christmas!

We all had the best Christmas we could ask for because Seth woke up in his own bed Christmas morning and woke everyone in our home with eager anticipation of what Santa had left him and Holly.  This year he also didn't even need us to call the hospital, so that's why it was the best.

Once school finished for the year, Seth and Holly got ready for Christmas and he even cleaned out his room.

As part of Seth's treatment, he collects "Journey Beads".  Currently his string is nearly 2m long.  Each treatment, he gets a bead.  If he has 5 days of chemo, he gets 1 bead.  If he has a blood test, he gets 1 bead etc.  If I have counted correctly, between Christmas 2012 and Christmas 2013 he has had -

73 Needles / port access etc,

23 Clinic visits,

16 Chemo Courses,

6 Lumbar Punctures,

6 Special visitors to hospital,

14 Finger picks,

5 Blood transfusions,

2 Emergency visits,

2 Hospital admissions,

9 Miscellaneous (physio etc.),

4 Scans,

PLUS he has oral chemo everyday and steroids for a week each month.

He is now in month 19 of treatment and is getting closer to half way (Jan / Feb 2014)!

So, although this isn't what I normally send, I hope the info helps and remember, Seth is one of many kids around the world fighting Leukaemia among other diseases and without the help of charity organisations like Koala Kids, Challenge, Camp Quality, Starlight Foundation, Leukaemia Foundation, Redkite etc. as well as the generous companies that work with them, Seth and all kids in Victoria fighting cancer wouldn't be able to do the beaded journey, go on camps, have wishes granted, have invites to movie theatres, dinners, go to the cricket and the list goes on ........................ To all of you, our friends, THANKYOU for your support, for not only Seth, but for helping raise awareness about Leukaemia and helping raise money so that the charities that help/helping us can continue to help through 2014.

If you're not smiling, why not, because Seth is

Simon, Nikki, Seth and Holly

P.S. The candle that Seth is holding was given to him by Koala Kids in a hospital admission bag they created to help kids settle into their hospital stay, the candle is donated to them by Enjoy Lighting Australia. The candle Holly is holding is a Christmas present from Seth, donated by Enjoy Lighting Australia. The candles are LED, battery operated and are hospital / baby safe, they can be cleaned and sanitized!

## <u>2014</u>

**15/01/14**

Hi,

If you're in Ol' Melbourne town, grab a icy glass of water and an icy pole!!!!

Since the last catch up, Seth has been enjoying school holidays and catching up occasionally with mates. Holly has loved the activities because Seth is currently ok to get out and about a little. Of course he's still having oral chemo, blood tests and hospital visits but his last blood test showed his blood results were good so he's caught a small pantomime at Westfield Fountain Gate, went to see Mickey's Magic Show (I think that's what it was called) and also enjoyed the small temporary pool in our backyard. Now we're in the middle of January, he is getting closer to "half way" for his treatment, very roughly he'll be halfway with chemo toward the end of January and start of February. We can now say that "All going well, he'll finish chemo next year" and I can tell you if you can keep a secret, not only is the light at the end of the tunnel getting brighter, psychologically it has made a difference too.

Seth is in grade 2 this year and Holly will go to 3 year old kinder from term 2 for a few days a week when Seth isn't in hospital ...... my baby is growing up into a big girl!

If you're not smiling, why not because Seth is,

Simon, Nikki, Seth and Holly


P.S. If you're approaching or over 50, please do not wait until you are thirsty before drinking (Melbourne is over 40 degrees Celsius at the moment)! I can't remember its name, but the part of your brain that signals for thirst, in a way wear out as you age and is not accurate once you reach 50. Please get a container and fill it with water and judge that you've drunk enough by what's in the container, not by your thirst.


**23/01/14**

Hi,

So far so good! Seth has been enjoying his holidays. Next Wednesday he starts back at Kung Fu and it's also Nikki and my 9th wedding anniversary which means a few weeks ago we had our 18th anniversary. Holly's dancing is also about to start for the year and she can't wait, she's twirling and skipping at any chance she gets. It also means Nikki's dance classes start again. I am still un sure how Nikki keeps Seth and Holly entertained, when needed getting Seth to school, Holly to dancing, Seth to blood tests and hospital appointments, Kung Fu and so much more. Then, she managed to finish her business certificate and just when I thought she'd take a break, decided to start with Body Shop at home.

This week Seth had chemo via Lumbar Puncture and then via I.V. Three or four hours later he was enjoying cooling off under a sprinkler. It also means he has steroids until Monday morning. At the moment he is taking 8 tablets twice a day, minimum and in true Seth style, he just takes them and then gets on with whatever he was doing.

This afternoon we all had an amazing time meeting Scotty Cam. He spent half an hour with us, showing us around The Block and telling us little bits here and there. We all think The Block is fantastic and will be interesting to watch!!! Scotty is a very nice, warm, genuine guy. I sent him pics of Seth's cubby (Seth's wish granted by Starlight Foundation) as it was being built to his Facebook page ...... the same pics I sent with my "Catch Up's".  It was very clear to me straight away that it was Scotty replying and not someone else on his behalf.  From there I'd tell him a little about us and then recently he organised for us to meet him today.  All without commercial camera's, no charities, no businesses, no person from the show telling him to do it, just Scotty himself.

If you're not smiling, why not, because Seth is,

Simon, Nikki, Seth and Holly

P.S. Some very dear and close friends have had some injuries recently, please give them a thought to help their quick recovery.


**4/02/14** – A note to his teacher

Hi

Seth's Neutrophil's are 0.75.  He will be away from school until mid next week.  The dr's have asked for him to have another blood test next Tuesday.  Depending on those results, we hope he will be back to school on Wednesday.  Also, his birthday is the 14th and last year he couldn't celebrate until March so hopefully he'll be able to celebrate on his actual day.

 Have a great rest of the week,

If you're not smiling, why not, because Seth is

Simon


**5/02/14**

Hi,

Seth went back to school and started to settle in, when ......... yep, his Neutrophil's are currently at 0.75, so it's safer to keep him at home until they lift, they are his immunity to any disease and need to be over 1.0 to be considered safe for Shopping Centre's, crowds etc.  So he had 2 days of grade 2 and is now back home.  He'll have another blood test on Tuesday, then each Tuesday until they lift again.  If they drop to or below 0.50, his chemo will be stopped.  It means he will miss out on a mate's birthday party on Saturday; a trip to Silvers Circus on Sunday and it's looking like (just like last year) he will be having a quiet birthday late next week.

Holly is loving him being home because she missed him!  Holly and Nikki have started their year of dancing this week and both are loving it.

It's short and sweet this week.

If you're not smiling, why not, because Seth is,

Simon, Nikki, Seth and Holly


**12/02/14**

Hi all,

Today's blood results came back and his Neutrophil's are 0.2 which means oral chemo is stopped until he recovers.

Then he got a headache so had a nap.  When he woke, his headache had gone but he had a sore tummy and his temp hit 38.  38 is a warning of infection and because his Neutrophil's are so low, he and Nikki have gone up Wellington Rd to Monash.  It looks like he'll be spending his 7th birthday on Friday in hospital.  In true Seth form, he told me "It's ok Dad, because we can still spend the day together."

So, unfortunately I don't have good news that he's off to school, but as I always say and write......
If you're not smiling, why not, because Seth is,
Simon, Nikki, Seth & Holly


**13/02/14**

Hi,
Seth is HOME!!!!!!!!!!!!!!!!!!!!!!!!!!!!!!!!!!!!!!!!!!!!!!!!!!!!!!
He is still neutropenic (very low immunity to infection) and off oral chemo.  He will not be able to have a big birthday party but a few mates will come over for a quick song titled "HAPPY BIRTHDAY" and a slice of cake.  He will have a blood test on Sunday and back for IV chemo on Monday and 5 days of steroid!!!  The steroid will boost him back up so he'll be back to school soon.
The pic was taken with us being silly in hospital before breakfast this morning, I got the best birthday present ever with him coming home today and he gets to wake up tomorrow on his 7th birthday in his own bed.
If you're not smiling, why no, because Seth is,

Simon, Nikki, Seth and Holly

**19/02/14** – A note to his teacher

Good morning,
Seth is getting dressed into his school uniform.  He will have a half day today to see how he goes with energy etc.  His Neutrophil's are still low, but the Dr's have suggested/recommended he goes.  The nurse from the hospital will come to school and give him his IV antibiotic, she will need use the "sick bay".
Hopefully this is the start of a good year for him!
Simon

60

**19/02/14**

Hi,

As you know, Seth was taken to hospital last Wednesday night. He had IV antibiotics and came home Thursday morning. Friday morning he woke on his birthday in his own bed and spent the day playing games he got for his birthday on out Wii U and watched a movie. One of my cousins came over and Seth had a great time showing him how to play the game, Holly loved watching her brother and in between playing with her doll house, she played with Seth. Seth even gave her a controller at one stage and Holly thought she was playing the game that Seth was controlling while standing behind her. After dinner, some of Seth's school mates came over for an hour to sing Happy Birthday and he loved seeing them, especially playing in his backyard and on his cubby! Saturday morning we were finishing breakfast and thinking about what to do for the day, then the phone rang and it was a Dr from the hospital. Seth has developed an infection whilst in hospital and needed to go in for IV antibiotics, 3 times, 12 hours apart. Off we went back to Monash, he had the 1st dose and we came home. After dinner, he and I went back and spent the night to have more at midnight and then 12pm on Sunday. This morning he went back to school for a few hours to socialise and start to settle into his new classroom and classmates because he had only been to school for 3 days so far this year. Holly has been enjoying Seth being home and when he goes to school, she keeps asking to go get him. She is loving being back at dancing and is always dancing up and down the hallway.
The hospital literally just rang!!!!!! The blood taken on Sunday has come back clear of infection. That means tomorrow afternoon, the nurse will come to our home and give him 1 last dose of antibiotic and take more blood that was originally scheduled for Friday ...... then they'll take out the cannula so he will not have a tube hanging out of him, he's very happy because that means he can have a bath tomorrow night, rather than a shower. It also means that his blood levels are lifting and soon he'll be back on oral chemo, oh yeah, he went to the Children's Cancer Centre on Monday and had IV chemo, antibiotic and check up. Unfortunately we couldn't go to Koala Kids annual event last Thursday that celebrates both donors and donees. We also couldn't go to my mum's birthday party Saturday.
If you're not smiling, why not, because Seth is.
Simon, Nikki, Seth and Holly


**5/03/14**

Hi,

The infection has been beaten!!!! Seth had I.V. antibiotics at school too; he was very impressed that he didn't need to stay home to have it. A very big thanks to Trinity Catholic Primary School Narre Warren South, they helped the nurse with anything she needed, including the use of the "sick bay". Seth is enjoying being able to go to school; he's starting to come back out of his shell. The latest blood test came back at 0.81 for Neutrophil's. With direction from Seth's Oncology Dr's and his school, he's still going to school....... Miss Berryman (Seth's teacher for grade 2) is on germ patrol and talking to Nikki where ever there is a concern. He is also back on oral chemo; it had been a month that he hadn't had it. Somehow, we all managed to make it through another steroid week without any injury...... I have noticed that Seth now recognises when he gets upset and manages it himself. We also wanted to walk to raise money for Monash Children's Hospital, but we couldn't do

it. This year, they were raising money for new parent beds..... YAY!!!!!!!!!!
We're all disappointed that Silvers Circus was at Fountain Gate and we didn't get to see their show. We'll need to wait until late this year before they are back on this side of Melbourne. We did think about the possibility of seeing them in Ballarat and visiting Poppy, unfortunately we can't get there. Seth will have more I.V. chemo in a few weeks and without checking the calendar, he'll have chemo via lumbar puncture the week before Easter.
Holly has been loving her dancing and playgroup. She knows she's off to 3 year old kinder next term. Every time she goes past it (next to Seth's school), she tells the world "That's my kinder, I'm going there soon, when I'm frrrreeeeeee". She also takes her backpack with her everywhere because; she's a big girl now and needs to take her toys.
If you're not smiling, why not, because Seth is,
Simon, Nikki, Seth and Holly


## 17/03/14

Hi,
this pic is Seth with Sully Monkey (www.monkeyinmychair.org) waiting for his chemo. We have just got the results of yesterday's blood test & Seth is finally no longer neutropenic, his Neutrophil's are 1.3. All other blood tests that were taken a month ago & other tests taken 2 months ago have also come back all good. We are all very relieved to have good news.
Seth and Holly have been enjoying their sport, Seth - Kung Fu and Holly - Dancing. We have discovered that Seth doesn't need physio because the Kung Fu is maintaining his core and leg fitness / strength. Holly is amazing to watch, seeing her natural balance around the house is brilliant. Last Saturday Seth and I went to see a mate shave his hair for Worlds Greatest Shave. Stu raised approximately $900 for the Leukaemia Foundation. Then we went to Relay for Life in Berwick where some friends where taking part in the 24 hour walk. Another mate named Stu managed to cover 56km's in about 22 hours and said that he walked through his pain because cancer is a lot more painful, his team raised over $6,100 and the total is still climbing because the total for the silent auction hasn't been confirmed. Stu was raising money for Prostate Cancer research.
So, Seth is now out of isolation and go to shopping centres and supermarkets within reason and we don't need to worry as to whether he'll get an infection. He still can, but being over 1.0 is a little less of a chance. It also means he can eat processed food again and ham that has been off the bone more than two days, twiggy sticks is one of his faves so he'll be able to have some again (note to self, go to the and get some).
Also, Nikki is enjoying her dancing; talk has already started about the end of year concert too.
If you're not smiling, why not, because Seth is,
Simon, Nikki, Seth and Holly
P.S. A little short and sweet this week.

**27/03/14**

Hi all,

I discovered that the last update I sent had a different pic than what was planned. That pic was Seth sitting on a couch in the Children's Cancer Centre at Monash Hospital, waiting for his chemo. The pic I planned to send is today's pic. It was taken on 15/03 at Relay for life Berwick.

Since my last update, Seth has had a blood test and his Neutrophil's are rising. Last weekend we went to Geelong Adventure Park with thanks to Camp Quality and had a great afternoon. Holly is loving dancing and apparently, she's talking to people at her Playgroup and being very helpful when it's time to pack up. I was asked recently what hobby I have and to update with this e-mail, well I don't have time for a hobby. With work and running around with the kids on weekends, I don't have time........ Maybe soon (after cure) I'll start a VW Beetle (50's or 60's model) with Seth and Holly; it won't be an ordinary Beetle when I'm finished with it. Seth has already shown me what it should look like when it's finished and he's spot on!

Not too much to tell you about this time around, always bits and pieces to add, but of course my brain has gone blank.

If you're not smiling, why not, because Seth is

Simon, Nikki, Seth and Holly

P.S. I'd also like to mention Telstra. They have gone over and above with something for us over the last few weeks and I'd like to recognise and thank them VERY much.

**02/04/14**

Hi,

What a week!

Seth had another blood test and his Neutrophil's are up at 4.7 that means he's immunity is high and also his oral chemo has lifted from 50% to 75%.

We had a fantastic afternoon with Challenge - Supporting Kids with Cancer on Saturday! We went to Williamstown yacht club and the kids went out on a boat cruise. Unfortunately there was a boat full of pirates that tried to attack the kid's boat. We were very relieved to hear that the kids and volunteers had a better strike rate with water bombs than the pirates and the pirates retreated. Nikki and I spent an hour or so talking to other parents on the deck.

Nikki decided that she'd sprain her ankle Monday night at her dancing class.  It was suggested to use crutches but is just hobbling around.

Holly's birthday is next Tuesday and she turns 3, so today she and Nikki celebrated her birthday at Playgroup.

Have a great week and weekend!

If you're not smiling, why not, because Seth is,

Simon, Nikki, Seth and Holly

P.S. Seth finally lost a 3rd tooth and it's one of the front ones!


## 10/04/14

Hi,

Holly had her 3rd birthday party last Saturday with a few friends.  It was a fantastic afternoon to watch her play and communicate with her friends.  Monday Seth, Holly and Nikki went to Enchanted Maze to have fun and also have an Easter egg hunt.... another fantastic day, thanks to Camp Quality. I spent my day of annual leave in bed, not with man flu, but trying to keep my cold contained to my bedroom, so hopefully Seth doesn't get it.  Tuesday was Holly's birthday!!!  She wanted to see kangaroos, so we went to Beechworth Bakery in Healesville for lunch and then Healesville Sanctuary.  Cold and Flu tablets, pain killers and energy drinks got me through the afternoon.  Holly loved her birthday!!!  OH!!! In the morning, Seth and I (and Nikki) got to watch Holly dance at long last!!!  We didn't see her or Nikki at their concert last year and it was so much fun, so enjoyable to see her smile, to see her bounce around the room, to see the anticipation for the next step in the dance was AMAZING.  A big thanks also to Naughty Nush Smash Cakes, I ordered a few things for Holly's party and when I went to pick them up, Jo and Romy had made a chocolate smash cake for Holly which she had great fun the night of her birthday, belting with a mallet to get into the lollies. Seth had a mate from school sleep over last night.  They finally fell asleep about 9pm and were up just after 6am ...... both kids normally go to bed at 7.30 and get up at 7.  Seth also lost another tooth tonight.  It's great because next Wednesday he has a Lumbar Puncture and if it was loose, the Dr's will just get pliers and pull it out.

Well, we've made nearly through the first week of school holidays and all is great, Easter is nearly here too!!!

If you're not smiling, why not, because Seth is,

Simon, Nikki, Seth and Holly

**16/04/14**

Hi,

Today Seth had chemo via Lumbar Puncture and then chemo via I.V.  Then, a bag full of meds to bring home which includes 5 days of steroid to start tonight and finish Easter Sunday.  We kept a special visitor secret from him today.  I organised with Daequon Montreal (A player in the SEABL - Dandenong Rangers Basketball team) to go to hospital and have lunch with him.  Seth met DQ and another player, Tony Lewis midway through last year's basketball season.  Both players live in the USA and make sure they see Seth as much as they can when they are in Melbourne.  DQ gave Seth a team singlet that he got all the players to sign and also season passes so we can take Seth to all their home games.  Unfortunately, while they were talking and eating sausage rolls (Mrs Es Rose' recipe) no one thought to take a pic.

Today he also had some extra tests done that he didn't like or want to have, but he did.  Also, Nikki told me he lost his smile a little due to the extra tests, DQ sure helped it come back when he walked in!

We have had a quiet few days and last weekend.  I am almost over the cold and Holly is loving Seth being on school holidays.

We hope you all have a great Easter and that Mr E. Bunny spoils you!

If you're not smiling, why not, because Seth is,

Simon, Nikki, Seth and Holly

**26/04/14**

Hi all,

On this "Anzac Day weekend" we reflect for what we have, for the lives lost and for those that have and are fighting for us still, without these people, we wouldn't be so lucky to live in such a great country!  We as a family have close contact with a retired serviceman that served to protect Darwin and a serving serviceman that has done Afghanistan many times in our family.  Both had/have served more.

We made it through Easter and the Easter Bunny spoilt Seth and Holly with an egg hunt.  Seth made it through 5 days of steroids and Nikki did a great job keeping him entertained.  Then term 2 started, Seth settled in straight away and loved changing his reader etc.  Holly started 3 year old kinder and on her first day, had her face painted.  I asked her what her two teacher's names are and she replied with a cheeky smile "Painter teacher" and "her teacher".  She has learnt their real names thank goodness.  Holly now loves kinder and of course playgroup.

This weekend has been full of playing and grass cutting.  We are catching up with friends this afternoon for Holly's belated birthday and Easter..... It's hard to keep 9 people healthy, if Holly and I weren't full of a cold, they were.  Tomorrow we are off to watch basketball.  It's the first time we have seen a game this season and we can't wait!!!!!

Someone I have met through Seth's journey let me know that he is a Dad for the first time!!!  Well done Jason and Judy, Jasmine looks beautiful.

Have a great week,

If you're not smiling, why not, because Seth is,

Simon, Nikki, Seth and Holly


## 30/04/14

Hi,

Seth started back at Auskick last Sunday.  He loves trying, Holly loves watching him.  We also watched the Dandenong Rangers men's basketball team win their game.  After the game, Seth was taken into the change room by the Team Manager.  Not sure what was said to him by the players, but he said they all said hi to him.

Last time he was in hospital for chemo, he had some tests he didn't like having, but in true Seth style, he did them.  Last night we found out that he has developed an infection in his bladder.  We are very pleased to find out that because his blood levels are high and including his Neutrophil's being at 1.6, he is on oral antibiotic and not needing to be admitted into hospital for IV antibiotics (the infection is also not too severe).  At one stage during the call, I expected Nikki to tell me he was going in.  Yet again, he keeps amazing me with his pain tolerance.

As most of you are aware, Nikki is taking part in "Stadium Stomp".  It is on 06/07/14, she will stomp on 7,400+ stairs at the MCG.  We are raising money for the Leukaemia Foundation.  Last year I did the "Speedo Dash".  We have registered a team "Stomping for Seth" and all team members (4 + Nikki at this stage) will wear red because it's Seth's favourite colour.  As at 01/05/14 the registration fee is $80.  Not one cent of this fee goes to the Leukaemia Foundation, so that is why we set up the fundraising page.  Not only do we get support, but they lead the research for a cure for Leukaemia.

If you'd like to join in, www.stadiumstomp.com.au is where to go to register; "Stomping for Seth" is stomping at 9.15am.  If you want to join the team, let me know and I'll send you the password, you'll need this during registration.  If you want to donate head to -

http://stadiumstomp2014mcg.gofundraise.com.au/page/SleepN?DonationGrid-size=30 .  Nikki is also trying to organise a fundraising night in June.  So far, her and Holly's dance school will provide entertainment.  Tonight we are hoping to organise a hall.  If you have contacts with anyone to do with catering or finger food, hire companies for tables and chairs and the list goes on, please let me know or pass on my e-mail address so I can contact them.

Holly is still loving kinder, she keeps telling me that she goes there by herself because she's a big girl.  Nikki has injured her ankle (again) while training at the 1000 steps in Ferntree Gully and the physio said to stay off it for 7 days, always strap it and yes, her particular injury is not a common injury.

If you're not smiling, why not, because Seth is,

Holly, Seth, Nikki and Simon

P.S. Tony is on the left of this pic, DQ (visited Seth in hospital) is on the right of the pic. Also, did you notice, Seth is proudly wearing his team signed singlet?

**13/05/14** – Two years since diagnosis

Hi Everyone,

Today is another big step for Seth and of course Holly, Nikki and I.

Two years ago today was Mothers Day and Seth had a blood test at our G.P. in the morning, we took him because we were concerned about a rash.  We now know that the rash was infact bruising because he had nearly no platelets in his blood so it couldn't clot.  That night I answered the phone and it was our G.P. telling me to pack a bag with clothes for Seth and either Nikki or I because the E.D. at Monash was waiting for him and he'll be there for "some time".  So we panicked, packed a bag and off he went.  I knew it had to be bad because about an hour after that call, which was 10 minutes after Seth and Nikki left for the hospital, the Dr in charge of paediatrics at the Monash E.D. called asking where Seth was.

Today, in true Seth style, he's gone to school this morning.  Nikki has just left to pick him up and take him to the Children's Cancer Centre for an appointment and his monthly I.V. chemo.  It also means that steroids start tonight for five days.  I want to explain the steroid - If your child has croup, they have (usually) 10ml per day a day of "Prednisilone" for three days. Seth has 40ml per day for five days.

Yesterday he had a blood test in preparation for today and then went to school. He has also started guitar lessons and it is going to help him with his fine motor skills. He has a tutor organised by Ronald McDonald House Charities, (yes McDonalds - the boxes on the counter and Big Mac Day etc.) to tutor him at school for one hour per week. He has O.T. appointments, organised again by RMHC every three weeks to help with his fine motor skills. Basically, he has a little trouble holding a pencil and writing for any period of time. Kung Fu is still going and he loves it, this is really helping with his balance and leg muscle strength, he will need to start physiotherapy again for a few sessions, just to help him a little. He still picks up his cricket bat in the back yard every now and then; he is also going to Auskick. He does the drills, but watches the game at the end to minimise the risk of impact.

Holly is enjoying kinder and dancing still. Nikki is still dancing and going to Boot Camp when she can ...... usually at 6am in the freezing cold!

Over the last two years we have met some amazing people. We have also been involved with many charities! I know there's going to be one or two people or charities that I'll forget to mention that have helped us. I am trying not to forget them, if I have please let me know!!!

I'd like to name everyone and thank you all individually, that's over 200 people that have in some way or another helped Seth and us, I won't but I will "name drop" a few people that have taken time out of their more well known life, ALL of you, named or not THANKYOU;

Mellie Buse - Producer of "Grandpa in my pocket"

Aaron Dragwidge

Amberley Lobo

Bobby Quiney

Michael Hill

Jayde Herrick

Cam White

Jay Laga'aia

Scotty Cam

Zigi Ozeri

Charities;

Leukaemia Foundation

Starlight Foundation

Camp Quality

Koala Kids

Challenge

Red Kite

Then there are all the "businesses" and "organisations";

Bearing Wholesalers (my work - without their support, I'd be a basket case)

Puffing Billy – Historic Railway

Zigi's Wine and Cheese Bar - Sydney

Cricket Victoria

Cricket Australia

Coles - Casey Central

Collingwood F.C.

Narre South Cricket Club

M&D Landscaping

Telstra

Last but not least Trinity Primary School, Narre Warren South - Seth's school.

The list goes on and on!!! In this, the hardest time of our lives, so many people have got behind us and helped, given us strength to continue, all of you a big thankyou from Seth, Holly, Nikki and I.

If you're not smiling, why not, because Seth is,
Seth, Holly, Nikki and I
P.S. Attached is a pic of Seth when he was first admitted May 2012 and a pic taken this Mothers Day at the Melbourne Star.

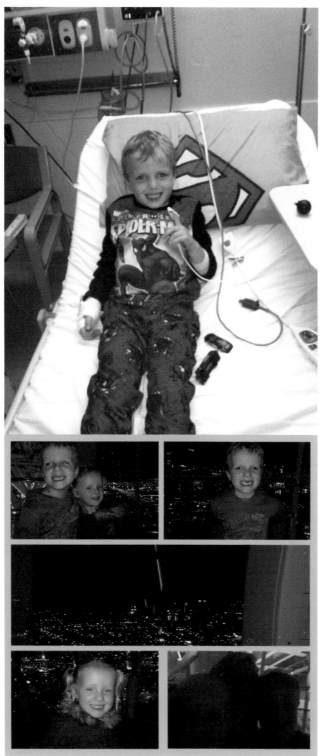

**3/06/14**

Good morning,
On this cold and wet Melbourne morning, Seth has gone to school.  He has an appointment with the O.T. just after 11am, so he'll go to that and then come home for a rest.

69

The last few weeks have been good. We went to Steavenson Falls near Marysville. Five years after Black Saturday and it's still scared. Lots of re growth, lots of re building, but they really need tourists to get back up there. We went there for 2 reasons, 1/ That's where I proposed to Nikki and we haven't been back since. 2/ Seth and Holly wanted to see a waterfall. There was also a trip to the Royal Children's Hospital recently to pick up supplies that aren't available at Monash. Seth and Holly loved seeing the Meerkats again. They were both excited to see the fish too, Seth was very pleased to see the fish he named Bob (In the pic) was still there. He also caught up with a few friends from Cricket Victoria on the same day, Seth had another blood test, chemo has stayed at the same dosage, 100% for his tablets.

Holly has a cold and Seth is showing some minor symptoms now (He didn't go to Auskick this week), we are keeping our fingers crossed that he can keep it away and that an infection doesn't develop. If it does develop, he'll be off to hospital for I.V. antibiotics and depending on what type of infection, he will either be admitted or a nurse will come to our home to give it to him each day. He will have another blood test on the Sunday before the public holiday and then Tuesday he'll have I.V. chemo. Mid July the treatment cycle starts again with chemo via Lumbar Puncture. If he stays on track with treatment and ultimately cure, that Lumber Puncture will be his 6th last one WWOOOHHHOOOOOO.

Holly has discovered Seth's skateboard and has decided that it's fun; look out world, here comes Holly!!! Nikki is dancing and busily training for Stadium Stomp, 7,400 steps at the MCG in July. We are trying to organise for Seth and Holly to go and see some the engineers (John and Tony, not forgetting Fleur and hopefully the ladies in the office) at Puffing Billy, Nikki is hoping to do it during the school holidays. He can't wait to see the workshop again.

If you're not smiling, why not, because Seth is,

Simon, Nikki, Seth and Holly


**13/06/14**


Hi,

Tuesday Seth went to hospital for his monthly I.V. chemo and 5 days of steroids started. As always, he did really well and came home full of smiles and energy. Then yesterday I received a call from Seth's school. They advised me that a child had confirmed Chicken Pox from his year level. Seth was already off school for the day because he's had a cold for a week or so and he needed rest. After confirmation that he played with the child within what was a contagious period, the hospital was called and a plan was put in place. I met Nikki there at the hospital and after a quick check with the Dr; a form was signed for the "special" medication required and with the help of the play therapist, Liz he was injected in each thigh. Straight into the muscle. In true Seth style, after some small tears, he and Liz continued on with their "Where's Wally". It must have hurt, although he didn't complain too much because he impressed the two nurses, but he would not give them a high five after they said he needed one for being so brave. Also, a big thanks to a charity, Koala Kids! After the injections he had a lucky dip and was so impressed that he got a Luke Skywalker key ring, it went straight on his school bag.

Now we wait. If he is infected, hopefully the medication and his own body's immunity will keep it away. If he does get it, hopefully it will not be a severe case. We now need to check his body temperature and look for symptoms.

Speaking of "Where's Wally", where was Holly I here you asking...... On the way to the hospital, Holly went to Kinder. She loves Kinder so much that she got to her room and apparently went about putting her bag on the hook etc. and didn't worry about saying goodbye to her Mum or Seth. Amanda, our saviour at times like yesterday afternoon, picked Holly up from kinder and took her back to her home. Holly had a ball playing with Taylah and Jacob, especially because it was it wasn't the weekend.

Keep your fingers and toes crossed that Seth doesn't have the virus and as always....

If you're not smiling, why not, because Seth is,

Simon, Nikki, Seth and Holly

P.S. Miss Berryman, please (I know you do anyway) read this to Seth's class and show them the pic, especially because it has he monkey with him.

## 13/06/14 – A message from his class

Hi Seth,

How are you feeling? We are missing you at school but there is a monkey sitting in your chair. Yesterday in Science we found out that some changes are reversible and some changes aren't reversible. Miss Berryman screwed one piece of paper up and then she set fire to another piece of paper. The burnt paper couldn't be changed back into paper.

Today we are celebrating Trinity Feast Day. We have just got back from celebrating Mass at the church. This afternoon we are joining with Mr Illman's grade to complete an activity. Miss Berryman won't tell us what the activity is as it's a surprise. We will tell you on Monday what we did.

We hope you get well soon, as we miss you at school.

From all your friends in 2B

## 25/06/14

Hi,

So far, so good. Seth is not showing any symptoms of Chicken Pox. He's now over half way through the incubation period, 1 week to go. He still has a cough but the cold has gone. He had a blood test yesterday and his Neutrophil's are 0.8. We now need to hope he doesn't get a fever, if he does, he'll be admitted to hospital. It also means no visits to enclosed public areas like supermarkets, shopping centres etc. Seth has also had a very big gap from Auskick and now school holidays are here, it'll be longer. He will also be in hospital the second week of hospital for one day as it's his quarterly Lumber Puncture schedule.

Holly had a big Asthma attack and spent nearly 3 hours at the doctor's surgery last week and nearly needed to go to hospital. She has seen the Paediatrician twice and is on Prednisilone (steroid) for the rest of the week. She also needs to have a "puffer" with a preventer in it twice a day and also we need to make sure she stays out of the cold until Winter is over. Thankfully, she doesn't need to have an operation as one of the "possibilities" was a condition that would need to be operated on.

Last week I also met Dave Hughes at a "panel" chat that was at a local golf club. That was a great highlight because I've always wanted to meet him. An even bigger highlight was finally meeting, personally thanking and shaking the hand of Jay Laga'aia because he was part of the panel as well. As you know, he has sent personal messages to Seth and is always up to date with his treatment. He is more amazing in person than he seems to be on TV! Next time, hopefully Seth can meet him too.

We were also involved with a fundraiser for Leukaemia Foundation last Saturday night. It is linked with "Stomping for Seth" where Nikki and 9 others are stomping up the MCG stairs in a few weeks. Final figure is not in because money is still slowly coming in. It is over $2,500 which isn't bad for a night out.

If you're not smiling, why not, because Seth is,

Holly, Seth, Nikki and Simon

P.S. Nikki is still going to Boot Camp and dancing, I don't know when she sleeps some nights.

**4/07/14**

Hi,

We made it!! Seth is now past the Chicken Pox incubation period and he did not get infected, EXTREMELY relieved is an understatement. The Dr's told us that if he did get it, it would only be minor. I am nearly over my cold and Seth, Holly and Nikki are getting round 2. Between Seth being neutropenic, getting a cold again and being on school holidays, he's sending himself and Holly mad. Holly is missing her kinder and dancing, so Nikki set up art activities and I think she may have almost worn out the DVD "Frozen" by now.

We are keeping our fingers and toes crossed that Seth gets over this cold really fast because he has a blood test on Tuesday. If his levels are too low, the Dr's won't perform his Lumbar Puncture on Wednesday. Ultimately, they will then test on a weekly basis until they are at a safe level to operate. If that occurs, it will mean that the final chemo month of October 2015 may change to November.

Stadium Stomp is on at the MCG this Sunday. "Team Stomping for Seth" have just about broken $5000 raised for the Leukaemia Foundation, between all the mums personal and group fundraising. If you can, please follow the link and donate, it will help families like us with support and of course the all important research to ultimately find a cure. If you can't, please don't feel pressured, finances are tight for everyone. To those that have donated in one way or another, thank you, not just from us, but from the Leukaemia Foundation as well. Nikki and the team are stomping 7,400 stairs.

Yesterday some of the team along with Seth and Nikki met Jo Hall from Channel 9, news. Jo is an extremely nice person and an article is going to air on Saturday night's news (unless something changes of course). The main focus is why Nikki and the team are stomping; there will also be some pics of Seth's journey. He also spoke on camera, but may not be used as he wasn't comfortable, IE; hands in his mouth etc. A rep from Leukaemia Foundation (Tennille) also spoke on air, so we expect it will be a great item to see. Renee, Jeanette and Tennille from Leukaemia Foundation went and met with everyone before the filming and then stayed after talking about Sunday, Nikki was nervous, but those three made her feel comfortable and also kept a keen eye and ear on what questions were asked, just incase a "curve ball" was thrown, Jo was very companionate and did not do that. They also made sure that if Seth can go Sunday, there is a room we can use for him to go into and be away from the crowd so he can still see his mum and the team stomp and not risk getting an infection.

http://stadiumstomp2014mcg.gofundraise.com.au/page/SleepN

If you're not smiling, why not, because Seth is,

Seth, Holly, Nikki and I

P.S. The pic is from Seth's last haircut. Andrew was a good person pre diagnosis, he has become a good friend and is always keeping Seth entertained. So much that Seth sees him between cuts and Andrew comes here sometimes.

**8/07/14**

Hi,

Over the holidays was "Stadium Stomp". 7343 stairs were stomped at the MCG (06/07/14). Team "Stomping for Seth" raised $6000 for the Leukaemia Foundation.

I wanted to share these pics because some of the team are mums at Trinity and wanted to support, not just us, but the Leukaemia Foundation too.

From school were:

Nikki Sleep - Seth

Amanda Mair - Jacob

Lisa Fabien - Taylah and Harper

Dianna Woolf - Melissa and Ryan

Celeste Vogrig - Dylan

As well as a few from our community.

I think that the pics show true community spirit and Trinity should be proud that they are part of such a fantastic community!

If you're not smiling, why not, because Seth is,

Simon Sleep

P.S. Yes, that is Jo Hall from Channel 9 news, Seth and the stompers were in the Herald Sun last Wednesday and on the news last Saturday night.

**28/07/14**

Hi all,

Firstly, thanks to those that send messages to Seth, he loves reading replies and finding out what people are doing!

Since my last update:

Nikki completed Stadium Stomp.

Seth did a grid game.

School holidays came and went.

Sovereign Hill visit.

We went on a family camp.

Nikki and team "Stomping for Seth" completed Stadium Stomp at the MCG. They stomped more than 7,300 steps and also crossed the start and finish lines together. Watching them finish together was fantastic, especially because they all wore red t-shirts because that is one of Seth's favourite colours. The teams combined fundraising total was just over $6000 for the Leukaemia Foundation. Just before the school holidays started, Seth participated in a grid game at the MCG. A grid game is the name of the kid's game that is usually played during half time at an AFL game. Seth's was before the game started and he had a blast. He didn't touch the ball once, but he ran around chasing it and had a massive smile on his face the whole time. As he'd just finished steroids, he didn't want to watch the game, lucky ...... we were at the Collingwood V Essendon game and Seth's Magpies lost. Seth was isolated at home during the school holidays. Unfortunately his Neutrophil's were less than 1. Of course they lifted just in time to go to school.

His school had a student free day the first week of term. As he'd been isolated and not been able to enjoy the school holidays, Holly, Seth and I went to Ballarat straight after school/kinder the day before his day off. We went to Sovereign Hill and had so much fun. It's been a long time since I was last there, it was great to see something I remember had not changed, but it is a lot bigger now, with more to see. I think Seth and Holly woke up their Poppy's house and I know their Poppy definitely loved every single minute we were there.

This weekend we went to the snow! We were lucky enough to be invited to Camp Quality's snow camp this year. It was Seth's second time at the snow. It was Holly's first time at the snow and first time on a bus. We stayed 2 hours from Mt Baw Baw at a camp and were taken on Saturday by coach. It is really good to be able to go on 1 camp a year with Camp Quality because all the families are either having treatment or recently finished. The kids have fun playing with each other and the volunteers are always nearby to join in or give the parents some respite. Of course there was more than enough food and family activities to be enjoyed. Even Holly had a go at Archery; she managed about 3 metres in distance with her arrow.

I'd like to mention that quite some time ago I was told about a prayer circle that our family has been included in. Thank you!

Also, in a few months (October I think), Bruce Haynes is attempting another world record. He is planning to break the record, breaking concrete with his hand/fist. Bruce has done it before and is an extremely well trained martial arts specialist. He along with a few others met Seth not too long after his diagnosis and made Seth a member of their martial arts family. We hope he breaks the record and Bruce, GOODLUCK!!!!

If you're not smiling, why not, because Seth is,
Simon, Nikki, Seth and Holly

**13/08/14**

Hi everyone,

After I pressed the magical "Send" button on my last update, I realized something VERY important had been left out!!!

HAPPY BIRTHDAY Nikki!!! She had her birthday while we were at Mt Baw Baw. Also, in the lead up, Nikki's oldest friend (back to kindergarten) Liz, along with her husband Andy and daughter Izzy came to Melbourne a week or so before for a quick visit. Liz and Nikki went on the Colonial Tram Car Restaurant to celebrate Nikki's birthday.

Since last you read, Seth has had few blood tests and a visit to the Children's Cancer Centre for his monthly chemo. He's also had 5 days of steroids and still takes chemo every night and other medications such as antibiotics twice a day, 3 times a week.....I still don't know how he doesn't rattle.

He also did his first reconciliation and went to a birthday party. Auskick has finished for the year and he has started to pick up his cricket bat lately. Sadly, it's a little damaged because he left it out near his cubby in the weather, but he still has a decent hit in him. Now, Nikki and I need to keep a very close eye on him. Last year and the year before he started to slide down in his blood levels. So much so that Christmas Day 2012 he nearly went to hospital and December last year, he was admitted for a few days. Then, he was in hospital the week before his birthday (got out the day before) and then the day after his birthday, he was back in.

This month last year, I and a few mates were spending our Saturdays building his cubby house. He and Holly loves it so much and Starlight Foundation, WOW, what a super "wish" you granted Seth. So many smiles, squeals, games and just plain fun has been had on that cubby, young and old.

Have a great week, Seth will have another blood test Sunday and then depending on the results, depends on whether the dosage of his oral chemo changes.

If you're not smiling, why not, because Seth is,
Simon, Nikki, Seth and Holly

**20/08/14**

Hi,

We've had a few things happen since the last update.

Holly fell out of a shopping trolley into a merchandise stand last Friday. Luckily she is ok, but has cuts and bruises on her forehead. We're still waiting for a copy of the incident report from where it occurred, especially as after the trolley tipped over, Nikki discovered it was not safe and asked for it to be repaired.

I had a rock try and replace one of my eyes on Saturday afternoon. It flicked up from under the lawn mower and I didn't have safety glasses on. I suffered very minor and temporary nerve damage that did affect my eye sight. I did initially go blind in the injured eye, but was able to nearly see fully within about 30 minutes, by dinner time, I could see normally. Today the irritation has almost gone and most of the internal bleeding has disappeared. The Optometrist did an extensive check, including a nerve scan.

Seth had a blood test last Sunday morning and his Neutrophil's have returned at 0.44. This means he will stay home from school to lessen the risk of infection.

He has also stopped chemo. He is Neutropenic when he's less than 1.0, chemo stops to give his body a chance to recover when he is less than 0.75. His next blood test isn't until September and he'll have a hospital visit the day after, I hope he doesn't get cabin fever again!!!!!! He is fighting a cold of some sort, his body temperature is very close to being classed as an infection starting and if he reaches it, he will go to the hospital for antibiotics via I.V. As his immunity is low, Nikki and I expect that if he does get a temperature, he will not visit, but be admitted and we think he'll be in for a minimum of 5 days. He's annoyed because he missed out on a school excursion to the Aquarium yesterday and book week is on at school next week.

Don't leave Nikki out!!! She got a bug that meant she not only missed boot camp yesterday, but she was in bed all day. Today she seems to be on the mend.

I think we need to get some cotton wool for a while :)

If you're not smiling, why not, because Seth is,

Seth, Holly, Nikki and Simon


**27/08/14**

Hi,

Seth spent the rest of last week off school. Holly loved having her brother home to play with. Wednesday night he had a temperature and so he and Nikki went to the E.D. Approximately 1:30am Thursday morning, he was sent home because he didn't have a temperature while there and the blood test he had after arriving came back with his Neutrophil's starting to rise compared to the blood test he had on the previous Sunday. Thursday afternoon he went to the Children's Cancer Centre for a check up. It was expected that he'd have a chest x-ray, but the doctors couldn't see any benefit as he didn't have any noise in his chest that aren't normal. Yesterday Seth had another blood test and then went to school. The results came back and his Neutrophil's are slowly rising. That also means he's back on oral chemo.

Tonight he went to Kung Fu. He and three other students were graded after the class. Grading does not occur until a student has achieved at least 12 months of training and is competent in all aspects of their training. As you can see by the pic attached, he's standing with Master Richard holding his certificate and black stripe that signifies he passed the test and is now officially a grade one Kung Fu student and no longer a beginner!!! Next week he starts training for grade two.

Sunday he'll have another blood test and I.V. chemo at hospital on Monday.

Holly loves her brother staying home and she was really good while Seth was at school on Monday because she has dancing in the morning, but she was very excited when he came home.

If you're not smiling, why not, because Seth is,

Simon, Nikki, Seth and Holly


**05/09/14**

Hi all,

We have had a busy week!  Seth has had his monthly I.V. chemo at hospital along with a few other appointments to help with some of the side effects of his treatment.  Along with the monthly I.V. chemo is steroids.  Tomorrow morning he'll finish his 20mg of steroid twice a day for a total of 10 treatments (5 days).  I think I mentioned once before, Holly had an Asthma attack and was given the same steroid as Seth, but was one treatment of 5mg.  That shows how much (just) steroid he needs to help his body with his fight against Leukaemia, and then there's all the other medication.  As an example, Wednesday morning he had about 11 tablets, then there's what he takes at night.  He's also had a lot of time away from school this week due to the appointments.  Somehow, he still manages to hand in is home learning journal ...... completed for the week.

Holly's bruising is almost gone from her fall out of a trolley a few weeks ago.  I asked her if she wanted me to get a trolley a few days ago, her reply: "No dad, that's a dodgy trolley".

Nova the cat is settling in well.  Astro is a little annoyed and every now and then sneaks up on him, but Nova aren't scared to attack back.  Holly also discovered Nova's "brother" on the new Dine cat food commercial.

Nikki is still going to boot camp and dancing in between the appointments, Holly even had an appointment this week.  She has been given the all clear and her Asthma medication has been reduced, which is great news.

I've just been trying to keep the grass cut without an injury; the safety glasses have been dusted off!  Today, Holly is enjoying the day with her brother.  As it's getting close to the end of term, Seth is getting tired.  We kept him home today to rest and his last appointment for the week is this afternoon, hopefully they don't get held up at the hospital and have to come home in peak hour traffic.

If you're not smiling, why not, because Seth is,

Holly, Seth, Nikki and Simon

P.S. This picture was taken by Nikki this morning.  See Seth's shopping list....

"Get snacks at Coles to eat at the hospital"

**11/09/14** – Note

Hi,

When Seth was diagnosed; he started a "Beaded Journey". Today he took it to school to show his classmates, the pic was taken by his teacher.

EACH bead means some sort of treatment! Diagnosis, blood test, radiation, chemo, hospital visit and the list goes on. The string is now approximately 3m long.

Thankyou for allowing me to work from home so Seth can have his treatment easily and Holly isn't either being taken to hospital all the time or being taken to a friend's all the time.

Thanks,

Sime

**10/09/14**

Hi,

I had an amazing Fathers Day; I hope all dads and special friends had an amazing day too!

Seth woke up a little flat Sunday. After some medication and a quiet morning, he perked back up to his normal self. Seth, Holly, Nikki and I enjoyed a few ball games in the afternoon. We also had two friends come over for a roast, Sunday night.

Seth is still low in energy and has had 2 days off school this week to try and recover. He'll also have a day off next week to help him recover more. Hopefully he'll be able to do some activities during school holidays too. He's been either in hospital or isolation every school holidays since he was diagnosed, May 2012. During the second week of school holidays, he'll have his quarterly lumbar puncture in the Children's Cancer Centre (about 4 left to the end of treatment hopefully). Last week he started for the first time in Grade 2 Kung Fu (after passing his exam the week before, he's proud of the black band on his belt) and Holly is preparing for her end of year dancing concert and also practicing her singing for the end of year kinder concert. He made it through a crazy week full of appointments last week ........... don't forget, he also had steroids, he is managing the side effects a lot better as he gets older. Although cricket season is fast approaching, he's still not sure if he wants to do it this season. Last season he only went to 3, maybe 4 sessions out of 8 in total. The sessions he missed were because he was either too sick or he was in hospital. His "beaded journey", which he gets a bead for each type of treatment, is about 3m long now. Seth didn't want a photo, I'll get one soon.

Have a great week,

If you're not smiling, why not, because Seth is,

79

Simon, Nikki, Seth and Holly

**17/09/14**

Hi everyone,

Seth has had a very busy week since my last update!

Thursday night he went to the E.D. had his port accessed and then had I.V. antibiotics, a nasal swab and luckily no temperature while there and high Neutrophil's, so he came home about 2am. Friday he went to the Children's Cancer Centre (CCC) for more I.V. antibiotic, a throat swab and a check up. He then had his port access removed because his Neutrophil's were high and his results came back as negative. Saturday, we had an early morning call from the hospital. The registrar called to say that one of Seth's tests had come back with an infection, so he, Nikki and Holly went back to the E.D. and was there for most of the day. He had his port accessed again and more tests and antibiotics. Sunday he and Nikki went back to hospital for the morning and had antibiotics on the children's ward. Monday he went to the CCC for a check up, antibiotics and test results. The results came back that he also has a virus and FLU. His Neutrophil's are also dropping and as of yesterday, he is neutropenic. He will have a nurse visit until Friday and depending on his blood test tomorrow, he should have his port access removed on Friday. Also, depending on his results, he might be able to go to school for the last day of term. Along with I.V. antibiotic, he still has an extra antibiotic tablet twice a day, with all his other tablets he takes.

I also managed to get the FLU and have been feverish and sleeping a lot since Saturday. I don't know how Super Seth gets through, I learn so much from him every day ....... he has a virus, an infection and the FLU all at once AND still wants to go to school! Luckily cabin fever hasn't set in from being home on him or Holly yet though. Nikki had to keep going in and out of hospital with Seth since last Thursday; they went 6 times, once each day Thursday-Sunday and twice Monday.

Yesterday, Holly got it!!!! She sat still all day; I have never seen her do that, even after her head injury a month ago at the shopping centre. Today she is much better and constantly improving.

The picture is Seth trying to play around this afternoon at home, while attached to the portable I.V. machine.

If you're not smiling, why not, because Seth is,

Holly, Seth, Nikki and Simon

**1/10/14**

G'day,

Seth and Holly want to give everyone a pinch and a punch for the first day of the month!!!

Since all the hospital visits due to infection and FLU a few weeks ago (his Neutrophil's are at a good level and so is all his other blood levels this week), Seth has enjoyed the school holidays so far! He even said they're the best school holidays ever. These are the first school holidays since diagnosis, that he's not either been in isolation or in hospital. He had a mate from school stay over one night and I loved hearing them chat.... they thought they were whispering. Then they were up early and I enjoyed having to ask them to be quiet so they didn't wake Holly. I don't remember ever needing to ask Seth to be quiet because he and a mate were up early.

Holly has loved having her big brother to play with. They've raced up and down the hallway, been to the Royal Melbourne Show, Aquarium and even the Tulip Festival. They also went and learned lawn bowls and rock climbing with Camp Quality. I was also lucky enough to have a quick visit at work by them a two other of their friends.

Today, Seth is having a Lumbar Puncture. To be confirmed, but today is either the fifth or fourth last

81

one!!!!!! Nearly 12 months of treatment left, October next year should be the month for Seth's last chemotherapy treatment. Then he's off down the Monash Freeway to the Royal Children's Hospital for an appointment this afternoon. The rest of the holidays are going to be jammed packed full of rest time!!! The pic attached was taken at school. It is his "beaded journey". He needs to get a few more now because he has visited the E.D., been to the Children's Cancer Centre a few times, had his port accessed, had nurses give him treatment at home and the list goes on.

If you're not smiling, why not, because Seth is,

Holly, Seth, Nikki and Simon

P.S. A friend of Seth's' Bruce Haynes is attempting to break his own world record for breaking concrete blocks, bare handed. GOOD LUCK Bruce!!!! We hope you "smash" the record in Adelaide later this month.

P.P.S. A big thanks to Seli at TVS Aquatics. She gave Seth some fish and fixed the lights for his tropical fish tank at home because he was so brave getting treatment and having all his medication while he had the two infections, FLU and was off school.


## 11/10/14

Hi all

Today is another milestone and tick in the box for Seth and his Journey with Leukaemia. Today marks 1 year left of chemotherapy treatment for Seth!

He is back at school and all tests are showing that his body is staying on track for October 2015. I wish I could say the last 2 & 1/2 years have flown, but they haven't. We as a family have made new friends, got closer to old friends and managed to raise some money for a few of the charities that have helped us with Seth's Journey. We have learnt a lot, not only about Leukaemia, but how charities work, how foundations work, how the Australian political system works and the list goes on and on. Seth will always be my Super Hero, what he has taught me is simply unable to be written. Trust, patience, understanding, pain tolerance is just the start.

Seth and Holly had a great school holidays! Now they are back in the full swing of Seth at school and Holly at kinder and dancing. Nikki has also gone back to dancing and will be working at a few events during the Spring Racing Carnival, including Melbourne Cup day. Today she has gone to get her Responsible Service of Alcohol certification ....... just to squeeze any last instance of time she might have had left.

Today as per the attached photo, we went to Seth's barber (Andrews Barber Shop - Beaconsfield) and Seth now has a new hairstyle. He decided it is getting too hot to grow it a little longer, so Andrew and Seth came up with this. Holly also got her hair braided by one of the hairdressers there so she felt included too. Seth had a big smile on completion. He quietly told me that he is happy to have a hairstyle back after losing his hair in 2012 and it not growing back until his birthday in 2013. Holly loves her "Frozen" hairstyle. Frozen (For those that aren't familiar) is a Disney movie, that is an animation and one of the main characters has a hairstyle like Holly's.

The next few weeks will hopefully remain uneventful and be "routine" with Seth at school, me at work, blood tests etc. Seth will also be due for his next Lumbar Puncture on Christmas Eve.

If you're not smiling, why not, because Seth is,

Simon, Nikki, Seth and Holly

**27/10/14**

Good morning,

Seth, Holly, Nikki and I have been getting back into normal "school" routine.  Seth and Holly handle it so well.  Seth has appointments, chemo etc., Holly has kinder and dancing and then she goes to a lot of Seth's appointments and they are both always smiling.  Holly and Nikki's dancing concert is coming up very quickly, a warning for me is when the tickets go on sale ...... today they went on sale.  Thursday night is Seth's school production.  They did one in 2012 and although Seth didn't know the routine, he followed his teacher and the other kids.  Last year the school didn't have one. This year his class is doing something with "friends", Seth is going dressed as Shaggy from Scooby Doo.  A few weeks ago, Nikki and I went to a talk at the Leukaemia Foundation office.  We finally had a chance to catch up with some familiar faces and also put some faces to names that we've spoken to, received e-mails from etc. over the last 2&1/2 years.  A few people weren't in the office, but we'll hopefully see them soon.

Yesterday we went to the Starlight Foundation annual "Extravaganza".  It was at Strike Bowling at Melbourne Central.  We all loved 10 pin bowling and laser tag.  There was also spray on tattoos, face painting, Captain Starlight hat making, balloon animals, magic tricks, a photo booth and food, so much food!!!! I think the best thing other than all the smiles on every single person face was a cheque for over $54,000 given by Strike to Starlight, it was raised throughout October and from their customers... The Captain Starlight on the advertising posters around the centre is one of Seth's fave Starlight Captains, Captain Rock-It, although she wasn't there yesterday, Seth made some new friends with Captain Confused and Captain Chatterbox.

Today Seth has had a blood test and will be heading into the hospital this morning for his monthly I.V. chemo.

If you're not smiling, why not, because Seth is,

Simon, Nikki, Seth and Holly

P.S. Well done to Leonie and her team and Marc and his team for completing the "Ride to conquer cancer" ride over the weekend that raises money for Peter Mac hospital.

P.P.S. Also a BIG get well to someone that has had a hip replacement and is currently enduring re-hab and all associated to get her moving around and making the most of everything as she always does.


## 6/11/14

Hi,

The last few weeks have been filled with fun and enjoyment. Seth has had a couple of blood tests and also had his monthly I.V. Chemotherapy and 5 days of steroids have been and gone. Holly, Seth and I even managed to grab lunch at the cricket club last Sunday. It was the first time this season that we've been able to go to the club, unfortunately because of bad weather early Sunday morning, the game was called off, but it was still good to be able to get out and watch Seth and Holly play hide and seek in between eating.

Holly and Nikki are madly getting ready for their dance concert in a few weeks and Seth is writing letters to Santa, it really is getting close now!!! He also asked me when I am starting our lights outside, I hate to say it, but I'll have to start after this weekend or it won't get finished.

Last week, Seth's school had their bi-annual junior and middle school concert. Watching Seth smile and love being there performing with his school friends was so special!

Of course the Melbourne Cup has been run and won. We enjoyed catching up with some local friends and our first Summer BBQ, even though we're not quite up to Summer yet.

If you're not smiling, why not, because Seth is,

Simon, Nikki, Seth and Holly

P.S. Thanks to Lisa from Enjoy Lighting Australia (Flameless candles) for our latest family pic. Last Saturday we finally met Lisa (and her family) after about a year of e-mails back and forth. Keep an eye on her Facebook page, there's a rumour that we may appear on it.

**19/11/14**

Hi,

Seth has had another blood test since the last update.  His levels are looking good and he'll have another blood test on Monday morning.  He'll then have his monthly I.V. chemo in the afternoon.  The list of recipients is growing for this update and I generally refer to "Neutrophil's" and what level he is, at that time.  He needs to be over 1.0 to not be Neutropenic.  Chemo stops if he is below 0.75.  Taken from "Understanding Acute Lymphoblastic Leukaemia (ALL) in Children, A guide for parents and families" published by the Leukaemia Foundation:

"*Neutropaenia*

*Neutropaenia is the term given to describe a lower than normal neutrophil count. If your child is neutropenic (neutrophil count of less than 1 x 10 (to the power of 9)/L they are considered to be at risk of developing frequent and sometimes severe infections. A child aged 5-8 years normal count range is 1.8-7.7."*

The definition in the same publication is: "*Neutrophil's - kill bacteria and fungi"* Also with the blood test, the specialists are checking his white and red cell count, as well as his platelets and haemoglobin.

Seth's last blood test came back with a neutrophil count of 4.4.  That is a little high and if he is the same or higher on Monday, his chemo dosage will be increased.  The chemo is used to re train his bone marrow to make non cancerous blood cells, if he over produces, he may re lapse.

What has Seth and Holly been up to?  Earlier in the year I contacted a V8 Supercar driver to see if he'd say hi to Seth when the racing was at Phillip Island.  Last weekend was that round and Fabian Coulthard did better than my request from earlier in the year.  Last Friday Seth, Holly, Nikki and I were given access all areas at the track and although I didn't take a picture, the passes we had said "Guests of Fabian Coulthard".  We were invited into his pit while "Tahllula" (his car) was being prepared for each practice session.  Seth even got to sit in the driver's seat!  I'm not sure whether Seth or Holly had more fun, Holly waved every time Fabian went down pit straight and he told Holly that he saw her and was waving back to her.  Fabian is an amazing person and was so good with Seth and Holly; we really had a ball and can't thank him enough for that day.  Dare devil Holly also went on the bungy trampoline.

Seth also had his Schools annual dance and for the first time since starting school in 2012, he went.  It was so good to pick him up from there and see in his face, how happy he was and listens to how much fun he had with his mates.

Holly and Seth then went to my mum's for the night on Saturday night.  Nikki and I were given tickets to "Taste of Melbourne" on Saturday night.  When we got there, we thought we'd walk around, have some food and go home within an hour.  Then the rain came and we went to a large marquee for shelter.  That was it, we met people in there that kept Nikki hydrated and we were entertained all night.  Scotty Cam was there and it was great to have a quick catch up with him.  Seth met Scotty a while ago and we were given a tour of "The Block" (the season before the last one) which was once a theatre in Sth. Melbourne.

Sunday we went to "Santa's Magical Kingdom" with thanks to a Melbourne based children's cancer charity called "Challenge".  We all loved it and it was also good to watch Silvers Circus again!

Then as suspected, trying to do too much and Seth telling us that he was ok ...... he had Monday of school and we thought he was getting a cold.  This morning he seemed ok and fully recovered.  We have one more busy weekend this weekend and then it's time to stop and rest until Christmas.  Last year and the year before Seth did not enjoy Christmas as he should be able to because he was too sick and both days we made phone calls to the hospital.  He wasn't taken there, but hopefully this year he'll be able to enjoy it the best he can, keeping in mind that he will have chemo via Lumbar Puncture on Christmas Eve and of course steroids.

This weekend is Nikki and Holly's dancing concerts!!  Holly is constantly "dancing" around where ever she goes.  Her 3 year old kinder concert is coming up too because she's singing "Santa is coming to town" as well.

If you're not smiling, why not, because Seth is,

Simon, Nikki, Seth and Holly


## 27/11/14

Hi,

Last weekend was a crazy, flat out and enjoyable weekend!

We went to Docklands on Saturday night and enjoyed Camp Quality's Christmas party.  Something happened to Seth when we got there, he rarely goes on rides and Saturday, he went on 2 scary rides, along with all the other rides ... Dodgem Cars etc.  One he convinced me to go on and I sooked up a storm, Nikki got off one almost crying and yes, Seth was smiling and wanting to go on it again.  We also caught up with a few families that we haven't seen for a while; it's always great to hear what they've been doing.  One Dad, I worked out last year was in my year 10 class, small world, his daughter has finished treatment and it is really helpful to get info from him as to what we can expect when Seth finishes his treatment next year.

Sunday was concert day!!  Nikki and Holly both had their dance concerts and it was so great to be able to sit and watch them.  Last year, Seth wasn't well so he and I stayed home and had to wait for the DVD.  Holly did all her dance class dances as well as group dances, 5...... YES 5 dances for little Miss 3 year old.  Then Nikki's concert was a few hours later and she did 5 as well!  We bought our tickets as soon as they went on sale. So we had front row at both concerts.  Being able to watch their facial expressions was brilliant!!!

Monday, Seth had I.V. chemo and 5 days of steroids started.  He has a cold and although his blood test results came back as ok, he needed to be isolated so he didn't sneeze on anyone.  That sent him a little crazy, but in true Seth fashion, he made the most of what he could to pass the time between appointments and chemo etc.

This weekend is the last of our Christmas parties (I think) that children cancer charities organize and Sunday is a quiet day at home.  Well, not for me, a friend has organized a small excavator to come over and work on our front and backyard to finally get the "run off" set properly so there won't be puddles anymore and also more importantly, get the land levelled so it's safe for little feet to run around and not fall over.  If there's time, I need to get the external Christmas lights and display up too.

Have a great weekend and enjoy decorating your Christmas tree; I know a few people have that

planned for Sunday.
It you're not smiling, why not, because Seth is,
Simon, Nikki, Seth and Holly


**04/12/14**

Hi,
Since my last e-mail, things didn't really stick to our plan, BUT we live with Cancer and that's what it throws at us.
Seth finished his 5 days of steroids.  We went to the Challenge Christmas Party and had a lot of fun.  Holly had her face and nails painted, Seth and Holly both went on heaps of rides and they each received a gift from Santa.
Late Saturday night Seth got sick.  Approximately 2am Sunday, he and Nikki rushed off to the E.D. at Monash.  He had tests and was put on antibiotics and potassium, along with other fluids.  He was also put on the ICU MET call alert list.  It wasn't called for him, but the E.D. put a warning into the ICU that Seth may need help because his blood pressure and heart rate were close to dangerous readings.  By lunchtime Sunday, he'd improved enough to be taken off the MET call list and was admitted up to the ward.  He had a few more tests while up there and spent a lot of time sleeping.  I stayed with him on Monday night so Holly and Nikki could spend some time together and also give Nikki a break because she didn't sleep at all Saturday night and only a few hours Sunday night.  Also, Seth asked for Daddy to stay with him.  By Monday night, he was nearly back to himself and hadn't been sick for hours.  Very early Tuesday morning, I got it and mid morning Nikki got it.  The Dr's did their morning rounds and told me that there was no infection or known virus in any of Seth's tests.  He had "Violent Gastro".  He was then taken off the drip and was under a 2 hour observation.  After he happily ate lunch, he was discharged and we went home mid afternoon.  We all had a lazy day on the couch yesterday to recover and Seth is at school today.  Tomorrow he'll have another blood test in the morning and then go to the CCC in the afternoon for a follow up.
While Seth was in hospital on Sunday, two of his mates, Pete and Dylan came over in the 34 degree heat and spread 2 metres of sand to help drain the backyard.  Hopefully this will help when the rain comes and he can get to his cubby a lot quicker than the few days it currently takes to drain and dry out.
Needless to say that the Christmas Lights didn't go up, but hopefully soon.
If you're not smiling, why not, because Seth is,
Holly, Seth, Nikki and Simon
P.S. This pic was taken just after he was un hooked from the drip on Tuesday morning.

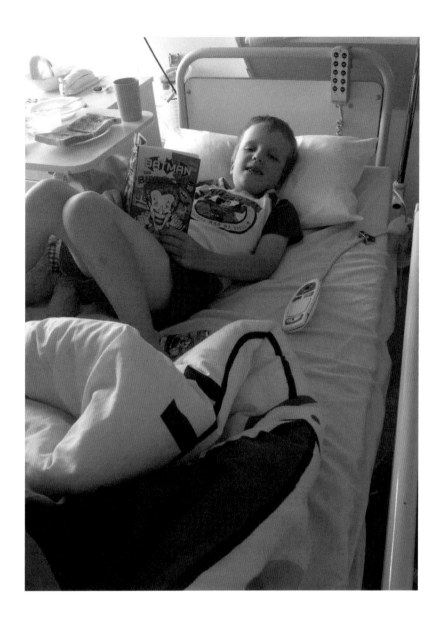

**11/12/14**

Hi,

Seth has been going to school and Holly has been to kinder and also had her Christmas break up at Playgroup yesterday.  It was also Holly's last Playgroup ever because next year she'll go to 4 year old kinder.  Saturday we saw "Paddington" at the cinema, it was a fun movie!  Holly had her trophy presentation on Saturday night for her dancing and Nikki worked at a private function that was at Flemington Racecourse.  Sunday, Seth went to a mates 8th birthday celebration at the cinema, I love when he does stuff like that because he missed a lot in 2012 and some of 2013 due to his immunity being too low or in hospital.

He also went to his first ever school athletics carnival!  The last two years, he's been too sick to even go and watch.  The smile on his face, the proud look in his eyes was something I'll never forget because he came home with 5 ribbons pinned to his chest.

Yesterday I took a day off work and went to Phillip Island.  I was lucky enough to be a passenger in a Porsche 944 Cup Challenge race car for a few laps.  We went over 210km's per hour down the main straight.  It was organized by Challenge - Supporting Kids with Cancer as a "Dads day out".  I have also got something in the "pipeline" for Seth that Jim, the owner of the race car is organizing with me for next Saturday (20th)...... No, Seth is under 16 so it's not anything to do with the race car,

you'll have to watch this space to see.
If you're not smiling, why not, because Seth is,
Holly, Seth, Nikki and I


**21/12/14**

Hi,
Three year old Kinder is finished for Holly and Grade 2 is finished for Seth. Seth came home with a great report and we are VERY proud of his achievements to not only keep up, but be higher than average with his schooling. He had 35 full days off school due to being unwell, they don't include public holidays, school holidays etc. They also don't include all the 1/2 days he had due to tests, appointments etc. His Ronald McDonald House Charities tutor also sent home a brilliant report. Kung Fu has finished for the year and he can't wait to get back to train for his level 3 exam late next year. This year he had a lot of Physio appointments and O.T. appointments because his fine motor skills have been affected by his chemotherapy. With the help of exercise, Kung Fu and Seth's determination to get better, he no longer needs to go to the physio and the O.T. is now changing her direction of treatment with him. Seth has had a blood test since the last update and his Neutrophil's (Immunity) were 1.7; hopefully his next blood test on Tuesday comes back with a similar result which will then (hopefully) mean he won't be sick on Christmas Day. Last year and the year before he was very unwell and although he didn't visit the E.D. phone calls were made and medication was suggested and helped to keep him home on Christmas Day. Christmas Eve he will have chemo via Lumbar Puncture and 5 days of steroids will start.
Remember in the last update I said that something exciting was planned for Seth and I? You may remember me writing about the day I went to Phillip Island and went in a Porsche Cup Challenge race car........ The person that I went on the track with owns a Lamborghini Gallardo. He drove the car to the track that day and I was able to sit in it for a photo. Since then Jim offered the key to me to take Seth for a drive. Not around the block, for two hours. Seth didn't want to cruise to the peninsula or along the bay; he wanted to show some mates the "Hot Wheels" car. We spent our time driving around to a few of his mates homes, we had lots of people on the side of the road and in traffic looking, giving thumbs up and kids on bikes yelling out "cool car". Seth told me that he will be the coolest kid at school next year because of the "Really cool Lambo". He didn't want to take it back, so much so that he went to a mate's house while Nikki and I took it back. Facebook, multi media in general is a funny thing because it was "tagged" on our trip to return it, you really can't go anywhere (not that it stands out and it's a metallic orange Super car at all). It was also surprisingly easy to drive. Jim told me "....it can be driven like a Hyundai". Other than the 5.0L V10 being loud, it was so easy to drive in traffic and around our estate.
If you're not smiling, why not, because Seth is,
Seth, Holly, Nikki and I

**24/12/14**

Hi,
Seth had his monthly I.V. chemo, Lumbar Puncture chemo and 5 days of steroids started.  His immunity is good, all other blood levels are good and he is enjoying a relaxed Christmas Day with us at home today.  The last 2 Christmas's he has almost been admitted into hospital due to being ill; it is so wonderful to watch Holly and Seth playing with their presents from Santa!
We hope you are all having/had a great Christmas!
If you're not smiling, why not, because Seth is,
Simon, Nikki, Seth and Holly
P.S. I think Seth likes the orange Lamborghini Gallardo's because he made a convertible version out of his Lego this morning.

## 2015

**2/01/15**

Hi,
We made it to 2015!

90

If all stays on track (I have everything crossed), Seth will have his last Chemotherapy THIS YEAR!!!!! Hopefully this Christmas will be Chemo free. He will then start 10 years of checkups, I think he'll still have monthly visits to the CCC for a while and they'll slowly taper off as he gets further from his fight with Leukaemia. We are by no means there yet, but we hope and we pray to get there.

We got through another steroid treatment without too many melt downs and no bruises. Seth has learnt how to recognise the signs of the side effects now and does a fantastic job to stay calm.

We had a great New Years Eve. Seth enjoyed New Years Eve until about 12:45AM New Years Day, Holly was asleep before 9pm. He was very excited that he was well enough to go to a friend's place to celebrate (He wasn't well enough the last 2 years) and even more excited when it was 12am!!!

A few days ago we went for a ride around the lake at the Berwick Springs Estate. It was about 2.75 Km's and was Seth's first long ride without training wheels and on his new bike. He had a little stack and grazed his knee, but was all smiles when we were loading the bikes back on the bike rack.

He was also impressed that his P.E. teacher, Mrs Charman saw us just as we were about to set off and she told him how cool his new bike was. Holly had the comfort of sitting in her seat on the back of my bike, while I did all the work.

Seth and Holly (I have trouble believing my own eyes, Holly is only 3, she's 4 in April and is riding without training wheels) have been madly riding their bikes around our court and also playing under the sprinkler and on the Slip and Slide when they're hot. Nikki and I need to keep an eye on the clock because Seth can't be in the sun too long (whether he's clothed or in bathers) due to his skin being more sensitive to UV than normal which is caused by his antibiotics.

This morning while I am at work, they went on another 2.75 Km ride around our estate before it got too hot. Nikki said that it was funny to watch them ride because they kept nearly riding into each other.

Seth will have another blood test on Monday. I will also try and collate all of Seth's blood tests, procedures, E.D. visits etc. for 2014 and let you know in the next update........ Hopefully!!!

Next week I am having a week off work and can't wait to spend the whole week with Seth, Holly and Nikki.

Nikki and I also passed a "milestone" a few days ago, we met 19 years ago on the 30/12 and we went out for the first time 05/01. Late January will be our 10th wedding anniversary..... Some will remember these dates, others we have met since.

If you're not smiling, why not, because Seth is,

Simon, Nikki, Seth and Holly!


**14/01/15**

Hi,

We all had a great few days at Balnarring. We all came back refreshed and happy.

Seth and Holly have been riding their bikes, doing jig saw puzzles, drawing pictures and enjoying the cubby as well. Seth has had blood tests in between having fun and of course, always with a smile. Next week he'll have his monthly Lumbar Puncture.

Holly has about 2 weeks until Kinder starts and Seth has about 2 & 1/2 weeks until Grade 3 starts. Holly is also looking forward to starting dancing again. She is going to a different dance school than where she went for the last two years because she is getting very good and the new dance school offer more opportunity as she gets older ..... If she wants to do more. Seth is looking forward to getting back to Kung Fu and is aiming to get his 2nd grading toward the end of the year.

I collated Seth's "Beaded Journey" and between Boxing Day 2013 and Christmas Day 2014 he had the following treatment:

53x Cannula's (Blood tests, Port Access, etc.)
20x Clinic visits (to the Children's Cancer Centre)

5x Lumbar Punctures (Chemo into his spine)

12x Chemo treatments (Monthly I.V. chemo)

2x Tests (nasal swabs etc. ....... 1 bead is for 1 infection, he had something like 5 or 6 tests for each infection)

5x Emergency Department visits

3x Special friends visits with him to the CCC

3x Hospital Admissions (Approximately 5 days each admission plus tests etc.)

6x Miscellaneous

1x Dentist

Then there's 5 days of steroids once each month, the daily chemo, antibiotics twice a day - 3 times a week etc.

This pic is Seth's Beaded Journey since he was taken to the E.D. Mothers Day (13/05) 2012, it is nearly 3m long (the ruler is a 1m ruler). It starts with his name and ends with the round bead that has a "Christmas Tree" on it.

If you're not smiling, why not, because Seth is,

Holly, Seth, Nikki and Simon

P.S. This is the first school holiday period since diagnosis, that Seth has not been in hospital, isolation or both and is also the first that he hasn't needed to rest everyday or felt unwell in his stomach. Hopefully he will continue to enjoy this break and all in the future!!!


**19/01/15** - A note

Hi,

This is what showing dedication does. Seth "put in" and HARD!!!!!! There are and were days (last year) he just felt pain while training, but still fought through.

I called and then wrote a letter to Master Richard to thank him for his understanding with Seth, to thank him with his and the other instructors input to helping Seth not only become the boy he is, but helping him to beat Leukaemia, to beat bloody CANCER.

With my permission, Master Richard has posted my letter (written last year) on their web page and e-mailed it to all the Golden Lion students.  Master Richard also told me during our phone call that Seth had inspired him; Seth had helped him to become a better instructor.

Martial Arts is not creating a violent person, Martial Arts is inspiring its students to become better people.

If you're not smiling, why not, because Seth is,

Simon


**3/02/15**

Hi all,

Seth has started grade 3 and Holly has started 4 year old kinder!!!

Since my last update, Seth has had a blood test or two and also a visit to the CCC (Children's Cancer Centre).  He had his monthly I.V. chemo and he made it through 5 days of steroids.  Tomorrow he'll have another blood test to check the levels of his blood and depending on the results, depends if his chemo gets adjusted.  He now has eight I.V. chemo treatments and three Lumbar Punctures left if he stays on track with his treatment.  He has also gone back to Kung Fu.

His eighth birthday is a week and a half away and he is getting very excited because he feels good.  This time last year and the year before he was not very well.  Infact, he was admitted into hospital for a week and discharged the day before and then the phone rang and he was re-admitted the day after his birthday last year.

Holly has also started back at dancing.  This year she is at a different dance school than where she went the last two years.  She told me that it was lots of fun and she can't wait to go back next week.  When I asked her what was the best part of kinder, she replied with "outside".  When I asked if she ate, she replied with "I was made to sit down inside and eat, so I ate all my food and went back outside".  I assume she likes the climbing obstacles and swing etc. at kinder.

If you're not smiling, why not, because Seth is,

Simon, Nikki, Seth and Holly

P.S. I don't think Holly wanted to let her big brother go back to school.

**11/02/15**

93

Hi,

Valentine's Day is nearly here and that means Seth is nearly 8. Saturday he'll wake up an 8 year old. Holly told me that she wants to make him a birthday card at kinder, I am not sure if she'll remember.

His last blood test results came back all good and his next I.V. chemo is next week, which means another blood test too.

We've enjoyed a few of his mate's birthday parties. He was very excited to go indoor Go Karting last Saturday at Chirnside Park for one birthday party and then outdoor Go Karting at Dandenong South on Sunday at another party.

Saturday was like pulling on an old glove ("Mrs R" I did something). Holly was meant to go karting with me in a double kart but didn't like the full face helmet, so I swapped to a kart by myself and cruised around the track while 5 other karts (kids and a double kart) raced around. I loved being able to get next to Seth on the track and see determination and excitement in his eyes (The pic attached is Holly watching me chase Seth on the indoor track). Sunday he had two 10 minute sessions. He improved a lot in the second session after a few pointers ......... he did however decide to ignore some of the "marshals" signals and crashed three karts at once. After that the kids went to Laser Tag.

He Is enjoying being at school, but today's forecast is 36 degrees, he doesn't like it when it's hot because he needs to sit quietly and play and not go into the sun because one side effect from his antibiotics is that he is sensitive to UV. Holly is bringing home picture after picture from kinder, I forgot that Seth did the same thing. Although the first impression of her drawing is coloured scribble, when she explains the pic, I can make it out..... She does a great drawing of Astro (dog) and Nova (cat).

She is also loving her new dance school and the classes she is doing.

If you're not smiling, why not, because Seth is,

Holly, Seth, Nikki and I


**19/02/15**

Hi all,

I love the "pool hair" and smile in this pic! ....................

As I write this, Seth is at the Monash CCC (Children's Cancer Centre) having his monthly I.V. chemo. That also means that 5 days of steroids starts tonight.

Last Saturday he had a pool party for his 8th birthday. We celebrated down at Blairgowrie (Thanks Mum and Max for the use of their pool, oops I mean home) and all the kids had a great time. His guest list was more than a mile long but unfortunately due to safety we had to limit the invitees. I didn't think it was possible, but it happened ...... his smile was just a little bigger all day than it is normally. This is his first birthday since diagnosis that he's not been in isolation and was able to really become a kid again and enjoy himself. Amanda (Amanda's Specialty Cakes and Desserts) out did herself again with Seth requesting a Minion cake with a beach theme (Chocolate mud of course, which is Seth's favourite.).

Upon his request, it was also my 40th party. I'm not too sure, but I don't think too many people can say they had a pool party for their 40th, although I didn't get in the pool. It was great to celebrate with Seth and all the mums and dads of his friends, along with a couple of mates.

Last week we also went to the annual cocktail party held by a small charity that help us and all the children's cancer families at Monash, RCH and also receiving treatment at Peter Mac .... Koala Kids. Last year Seth was not well enough to go, infact he was in hospital the night it was held, so it was great to get there this year and meet all the volunteers and some of the supporters. It was also touching to see a photo of Seth and Holly included in their montage presentation.

This week Seth and Holly both have a little sniffle and cough.  At the moment they both do not have a temperature and Seth's Neutrophil's (immunity) is above 1, so he will hopefully be able to fight it and not need more antibiotics or to be admitted into hospital for IV antibiotics.  Hopefully the next few weeks will stay relatively un eventful so they'll have a chance to beat off their cold.

Short and sweet this week, hopefully he'll be on his way home before too long and won't get caught up in the peak hour traffic.

If you're not smiling, why not, because Seth is,

Simon, Nikki, Seth and Holly

P.S. A mate of Seth's is shaving his head and beard for "Worlds Greatest Shave", which is to raise money for the Leukaemia Foundation.  Seth will be there at his barber, Andrews Barbershop in Beaconsfield to cheer Dylan on.  If you can, please follow the link and help with much needed money to go toward research and family support...

https://secure.leukaemiafoundation.org.au/registrant/FundraisingPage.aspx?Referrer=%26Referrer%3dhttp%253a%252f%252fwww.worldsgreatestshave.com%252f%253fgclid%253dCIWvj-WF7cMCFVcmvQodpioAkA&RegistrationID=563159#&panel1-2

**5/03/15**

Hi all,

Seth got through 5 days of steroids!  We did too.  Seth's school had a very successful carnival last Sunday to raise money towards raising the school oval so it's usable all year, I saw smiles EVERYWHERE.  I was especially proud of Nikki being a committee member and spending the day "at her post" with barely a break.  Seth and Holly had lots of fun with their friends.  I LOVED watching Seth interact with his friends and seeing his smile, it was brilliant to see him able to participate.  Today he had another blood test and although his immunity has dropped since his last blood test, it is still at a safe level to go to school and enjoy the upcoming long weekend.  Next week is the World's Greatest Shave to raise money for the Leukaemia Foundation.  Thursday night a friend of ours from Narre South Cricket Club is shaving his head and beard at Seth's barber, Andrew's Barbershop in Beaconsfield.  Dylan Wright and I (Someone from LF will talk to them on Tuesday to be recorded too) have also spoken to the morning crew at Star FM, Gippsland.... Mandy and Brad about the shave.  Dylan will be heard Wednesday morning and I'll be on air Thursday morning, all in anticipation for Brad to shave his head on Thursday night.  If he raises over $1000 he will also shave off his beard.

I will also be heading to Akoonah Park in Berwick on Friday and then Saturday to support Relay for Life. This year I'll be towing the equipment and helping set up the camp site and then Saturday Seth, Holly, Nikki and I will do a few laps with the team "In Loving Memory".

Nikki has also been flat out organizing our annual fundraiser to coincide with Stadium Stomp in July. Nikki and "Team Stomping for Seth" with be at it again this year, stomping 7000+ stairs at the MCG. We will have a fundraising bank account set up in the next few days and tickets are now available for Monday 13th of July at Village Fountain Gate, for an arrival time of 6:30pm to watch "Magic Mike XXL". Seats will not be numbered and are $30 each. Included is a small popcorn and drink. All profits will go to Leukaemia Foundation to be used for research etc. We will also organize a raffle and door prizes. Please note that Nikki has booked a cinema and the screening is for "Team Stomping for Seth" fundraising only, general public will not enter the cinema.

If you're not smiling, why not, because Seth is,

Nikki, Holly, Simon and Seth


## 08/03/15

Hi All,

Nothing at all related to Seth's Leukaemia is that he woke up with a sore tummy and difficulty with movement on Saturday morning. By about 11:30am he was in the E.D. and fasting for an operation. 8pm they told us he could eat because the op was changed to this morning (Sunday). Seth had his appendix taken out and it was inflamed. It is not good that he needed the op, but it is good the appendix was inflamed because that means it was definitely causing the pain.

He had an ultra sound, x-ray, urine and blood tests yesterday and still smiling!

He will be in hospital at least until tomorrow afternoon, but it is likely to be longer. He will miss school this week and hopefully he'll be able to go back the following Monday and then chemo via lumbar puncture that Wednesday. He will also miss Kung Fu for at least 2 weeks; the doctor told us that it's a 2-3 week recovery for non contact sports.

If you're not smiling, why not, because Seth is,

Seth, Holly, Nikki and Simon


## 18/03/15

Hi,

Since Seth had his Appendix out; he spent a week at home recovering. Last Wednesday night one of his class mates came over to see how he was and tell him what he'd missed at school. Seth was very humble when he found out his teacher had been telling his class about why Seth is away and what operation he had. He was also amazed that she had shown the class what and where an Appendix is. He was really happy that Sully was keeping his chair warm. Sully is a monkey (stuffed toy) with a school t-shirt on that does what the class does when Seth is away. Some are new to my updates, he came from an American based charity called "Monkey in my chair" and its main purpose is to help the class while Seth is away and Seth has a smaller version too.

Over the weekend I helped a little with a team at Relay for Life in Berwick. We also went to a friend's shave for the Leukaemia Foundation's World's Greatest Shave.... I was also on Star FM Gippsland last Thursday talking about the shave and Seth; it was strange listening to myself while driving to work because it was recorded to sound as if it was live.

Last Monday Seth went back to school. He was really happy to be back and had a big smile when I came home from work and he was telling me about the get well card his class wrote in.

He is at Monash now.  He has had his quarterly chemo via Lumber Puncture (If he stays on track with his treatment, today is his 3rd last LP) and will be seen by the surgeons that operated on him last week to make sure he's healing properly.  After that, he'll have more chemo via I.V. and come home.  Tonight he'll start steroids for 5 days and of course oral chemo tomorrow morning.

Tomorrow Holly has an appointment with her Ear, Nose and Throat surgeon; hopefully she won't need grommets again.  Nikki has her operation next Wednesday.  She will have an arthroscopy procedure to repair a tear in her Meniscus, basically a sporting injury in her knee.  That will mean she'll need crutches for a few days and can't drive for about 5 days or so.

If you're not smiling, why not, because Seth is,

Simon, Nikki, Seth and Holly

P.S. This pic is from this morning.  He was enjoying a snooze after his LP and as always Billy is keeping him safe, before he wakes for lunch.

**28/03/15**

Hello, hi and g'day,

Seth made it through 5 days of steroids after his Lumbar Puncture and although it affected him whilst taking it, he recovered very quickly once they were finished.  Holly got the all clear from her E.N.T. specialist; she doesn't need grommets again, but needs another check up in June to make sure her ear canals are developing properly.

Nikki had her knee surgery.  Pre op, the discussion was to have Panadeine and she'd be back on both feet in 5 or so days.  Post op, the discussion changed to 5 days before the bandages come off, 3 days of Endone (prescription only pain killer) and then try Panadeine and no driving for 10 days, it seems more work was needed to her knee than first thought.  She has been up and about a little each day and gets frustrated with the crutches and how long it takes her to get anywhere.  She should be good to go without them by Easter and back into training for Stadium Stomp a week or so after that.  We also met Giaan Rooney, former Australian Commonwealth Games and Olympic swimmer.  After briefly mentioning Seth's journey, she told us of people close to her and their journeys.  It was hard for Nikki to hear and I felt very proud when she said "Nikki you are an amazing mum and I find you so inspiring".  A former athlete that represented Australia so many times finds Nikki inspiring and yet we look up to her, wow.

School holidays are here; both Seth and Holly are already driving each other mad and loving it.  Seth will have another blood test just before Easter and then chemo via I.V. a week after.  He now has 2 Lumbar Punctures left if all stays on track, I forgot that he has I.V. chemo with each LP, so he has 7 I.V.'s left in total..... But who's counting?!?!

With Easter nearly here, Seth and Holly are hoping to be able to stay awake to sneak a peek at the Easter Bunny, Seth said he's seen him the last few years.

If you're not smiling, why not, because Seth is,

Simon, Nikki, Seth & Holly.

**04/04/15**

Hi,

Seth and Holly are enjoying the school holidays. Last Wednesday we went to the Enchanted Maze for an Easter egg hunt with Camp Quality. We all had a great day; Nikki did lots of hobbling and lots of sitting due to her knee still being sore. On our way home we saw three horses bolting towards us without riders, about 200m down the road were 2 girls (6 and 9) and 1 lady jumping up and down and looking like they were being attacked. When we got to them, we discovered that they were being attacked by a swarm of wasps. For the first time ever, I called 000, it was a little strange to do it, but the two girls and lady had bites all over them, almost head to toe. I spoke to a lady later that night that turned out to be one of the girls grandmothers and she told me they had been to the ED and were all home because they responded to the medication. Seth and Holly were brilliant! They stayed in the car (with the A/C on and within our sight) away from the danger and luckily they were far enough away to only see the police car and ambulance flashing lights, not the peoples bodies covered in bites.

Seth also had another blood test last Thursday and in true Seth style, smiled even though this time it hurt him and then we headed home. Nikki has finally been able to not use crutches today, she has gradually progressed form using both, to using one and finally today she has enough strength and minimal pain so can limp without any support. The bandages have also come off, but there is still strips and tape holding her skin together.

We hope you have a brilliant Easter / break!

If you're not smiling, why not, because Seth is,

Simon, Nikki, Seth & Holly

**17/04/15**

Hi,

School's back!!!! Although Seth and Holly loved the break, they missed their routine. Seth and Holly love getting back to school and kinder and of course Kung Fu and Dancing.

Seth had another I.V. chemo this week (as you can see neither Holly nor Seth wanted to smile for the pic), his monthly appointment. That also means 5 days of steroids have started!

We also went to an Engagement Party last weekend (Congrats Damian and Sandra!); we caught up with a cousin I haven't seen since June and another I've never met. Seth and Holly had a ball playing with the kids too.

Nikki's knee is still mending, she's started back at group PT under advice from her surgeon and he believes she will be ok to do Stadium Stomp at the MCG in early July. This year Nikki has booked a cinema at Village, Fountain Gate to see Magic Mike XXL for Monday 13th July at 6:30pm. Tickets are $30 each (The seats will not be number allocated, for an extra $5/ticket you can pick your seat and will also be escorted), the price includes a small popcorn and soft drink. All profits are to coincide with "Team Stomping for Seth" participating at Stadium Stomp (7,400 + stairs at the MCG) and the teams effort to raise money for the Leukaemia Foundation. We are also working on a raffle and have some great prizes so far. If you'd like to book a seat or six for the movie, let Nikki or I know and we'll forward the bank details to you or pay cash to us and then we'll send you the ticket/s.

REMEMBER all profits are for the Leukaemia Foundation to fund further research and one day find a cure.

During the holidays, Holly had her 4th birthday too. HAPPY BIRTHDAY H O L L Y ! ! She loved turning 4 and now tells us that she is ready for school next year when she turns 5.

If you're not smiling, why not, because Seth is,

Nikki, Holly, Seth and Simon

P.S. A very close friend lost her sister last weekend, she was nearly 98. RIP Eva.

P.P.S. Good luck down at Phillip Island racetrack Jimmy, go number 13 for Round 2 of the (Porsche) 944 Challenge.


**20/04/15** – A note

Hi,

I was at Sandown for a 12:45pm start. I cannot remember my instructor's name (I am sorry because he made an impression on me); I was in the Valvoline car that had "TIM" on its rear window.

The instructor was fantastic! I was a bit of a handful, but he got me through.

Upon re-entry to the pit he told me that he donates to Peter Mac every week, he told me after I thanked him for helping to relieve some stress related to my son being almost 3 years since diagnosis of Leukaemia and will hopefully finish treatment and begin a normal life mid October this year. Both Seth (8) and Holly (4) were there with my wife to watch.

Once the car had stopped, I pointed Seth out to him because Seth has had radiation treatment at Peter Mac as part of his treatment.

PLEASE pass on this pic to him; this is Seth and Holly entertaining themselves whilst I was waiting down in pit lane on the chairs.

If you're not smiling, why not, because Seth is,

Simon Sleep

**25/04/15**

Hi,

This week was a big week for Seth. He was well enough to go to his school's sports carnival, that's the second he's been to since he started school in 2012. He came home with big smiles and some ribbons. There is no doubting his determination! Not so long ago he was not able to walk without limping (especially when he was tired), not so long ago he couldn't write or draw for more than a few minutes before his pain was too strong. The chemo had eaten his muscles, especially the left side of his body. He went to the physio, he went to Occupational Therapy, he is learning to play the guitar and training the art of Kung Fu. As you know, he stopped physio earlier than expected and keeps on keeping on... He won first place in his race with some grade 3's in a 100m sprint!!!

Holly is loving every minute of kinder and dancing. She is always showing me what she did and learnt at dancing, even in the shopping centre to the amusement of anyone near her.

Nikki is about to start a part time job, it's been almost 3 years since she last worked, I think it's going to be a very big step for her.

I went to Sandown racetrack last Saturday. I was given a 4 lap drive voucher in a V8 race car from a group of friends for my birthday back in February. I finally got to drive around the track I've watched and also been a passenger on, it was better than I thought. It took a few laps to get used to the car and track but I did get the car over 210km/hr down the front straight. V8 Supercar drivers get their 600hp V8's to about 260km/hr.

If you're not smiling, why not, because Seth is,

Simon, Nikki, Seth and Holly


**07/05/15**

Hi,

Seth has had another blood test since my last update and yet another next Wednesday. I will sit down and work it out, but I would not be surprised if he's had 100 blood tests by now (That's in 2 years, 11 months and 3 weeks, but who's counting). His body is doing exactly what it needs and even fought off a sniffle last week! Next week will be his monthly I.V. chemo and of course the start of 5 days of steroids.

Holly is loving dancing so much that she's thinking about participating in a midyear concert... SOLO and self choreographed. She's getting better on her skateboard and has her dads need for speed on her bike ...... remembering what I used to do around Eltham, I'm glad it's not so hilly where we live!!!

Nikki has started her new part time job and is enjoying the new challenges. I'm now taking over more of Seth's treatments / appointments and I think she will miss that a little. My work have been far and beyond with their support for Seth and the rest of us, we have been able to incorporate Nikki's job and Seth's appointments around my work.... grateful is an understatement!

HAPPY MOTHERS DAY to all, not just mums by birth, but ALL MUMS!!!

If you're not smiling, why not, because Seth is,

Simon, Nikki, Seth & Holly


**13/05/15**

Hi everyone

Today is the 3rd anniversary for our fight with Leukaemia.

May 13, 2012 was Mothers Day, Seth had what we thought was a rash and an enlarged tummy. By 11am he had a blood test at our G.P. and we were shown that his glands were also up. The G.P. told us to go home and not do anything in public and if Seth hurt himself, we had to go straight to hospital because she did not know why his blood wasn't clotting..... The rash was infact bruising and his enlarged tummy was due to his spline being enlarged.

Approximately 6pm the phone rang and it was our G.P. She told me that Seth had to go to Monash E.D. in Clayton and the head Doctor of E.D. Paediatrics was waiting for him. I asked what was wrong, she calmly replied with "Seth needs more tests, the preliminary results are inconclusive, please pack a bag to be able to stay for a few days while the tests is done." I asked if he had Leukaemia, she replied "Please get him to hospital, they are waiting for him." That's the basics of the conversation and so Nikki packed a bag and off they went.

Lots of sleepless nights, lots of worry, lots of stress, lots of tests, lots of treatments, lots of special, lots of happy, lots of enjoyable, lots of precious times have happened since that first blood test and Seth has had another blood test today, the 3rd anniversary since he went to the E.D. and stayed there for approximately 2 weeks.

A while ago I thanked a lot of people and a lot of organisations for what they have done throughout our journey so far. I know I missed a few like Seth's school and Puffing Billy Tourist Railway, but there is also people who have recently come into our lives like Jimmy that loaned Seth and I his 2005 Lamborghini Gallardo just before Christmas with a full tank of petrol, an E-tag and from his mouth "Take it and enjoy it, go down the peninsula and have fun." A real once in a lifetime experience without the glitz and glamour of media etc. just plain and simple genuine caring person that wanted to help Seth.

Thanks to each and every one of you that read these updates, Seth also gets a kick out of reading your replies and so do Nikki, Holly and I.

If you're not smiling, why not, because Seth is,

Seth, Holly, Nikki and Simon

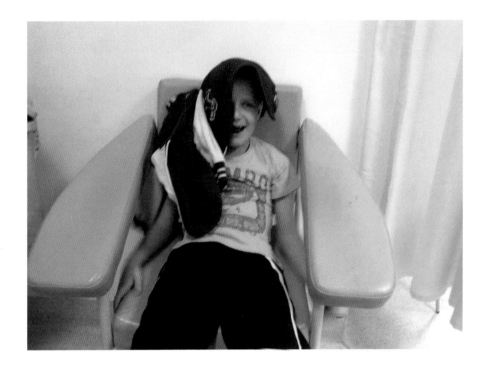

**28/05/15**

Hi all,

Seth has had I.V. chemo since my last update. On that day he went to school for NAPLAN, went to Monash CCC for chemo and back to school to do a 2km cross country run. He continues to amaze me, infact even his P.E. teacher was shocked with his achievement. For the first time since he got sick he told me to change his chemo appointment (he never complains) so he could do the run, instead thanks to the nurses, they worked with us to get him back to school in time, amazing kid!!! Today he had another blood test and for the second time ever, he was number 1!!! He was so pleased and he saw a nurse he hadn't seen in over a year whom remembered him, so he was very happy. The other nurse (he's never seen her before) was impressed when she asked if any help was required and the answer from his nurse was "No thanks, Seth is a Super Star and just does what I ask him to do."

Seth and Holly have finally discovered "Siri" the lady that answers questions on Apple brand products like Seth's ipad. It is very entertaining to hear their questions and very funny listening to the answers.

Holly is still loving kinder and dancing. She loves dancing so much that she asked to go in the mid year concert....... SOLO!!!! It's going to be interesting to see what choreography she comes up with and whether she gets stage fright or not.

Nikki is enjoying work and has a little extra bubble and spring at the moment; she is missing not going with Seth to all the blood tests and appointments etc. She's also spending spare time organising the fundraiser for the Leukaemia Foundation. Magic Mike XXL will be a very interesting night with mostly ladies buying tickets so far, don't forget that tickets need to be pre purchased from us and are not available from Village Fountain Gate's box office for the booked session, 6:30pm 13/07/15.

I seem to be the only one without a cold at the moment, hopefully I stay healthy but I did find my bed 7:30pm last Saturday night.

If all stays on track, Seth will have his second last Lumbar Puncture in a few weeks.

If you're not smiling, why not, because Seth is,

Simon, Nikki, Seth and Holly

P.S. To all holding or going to a Cancer Council Biggest Morning Tea, thanks!

**10/06/15**

Hi,

Today was Seth's 2nd last chemo via Lumbar Puncture.  The Oncology team are happy with all blood test results and said "he is doing exactly as we expect and want him to do".  He has had another couple of blood tests leading up to today and will continue with fortnightly blood tests.  Tonight is the start of 5 days of steroids too.

A while ago Nikki won a family pass to Sovereign Hill and every weekend we planned to go, Seth was unwell or recovering.  Last weekend we got there and had so much fun!  It was a little cold, but we still spent a whole afternoon there and didn't get time to do everything.  Dad's place will never be the same.... 5 adults and 5 kids for dinner Saturday night, the noise was brilliant, one thing from many out of our fight with Leukaemia is a true appreciation for noise made by kids playing and enjoying themselves!

Holly is getting ready for her 1st dance solo in a few weeks, I still can't believe that she is 4 and has worked out her costume (without shoes), song and most of the routine by herself.

Nikki is back to training and gearing up for stomping 7,300+ stairs at Stadium Stomp (MCG) in July.

There's also not long until school holidays, both Seth and Holly are looking forward to a rest and also enjoying time away from their activities.

If you're not smiling, why not, because Seth is,

Seth, Holly, Nikki & Simon

**29/06/15**

Hi,

The end of term 2 has happened and school holidays have started.

Seth did his guitar recital and did a great job.  Even though chemo has affected his fine motor skills, it was still clear enough to hear a verse of Old MacDonald.

Seth brought home an exceptional half year school report, we are very impressed that he has been able to keep up with his work and not allowed too many distractions.  We don't know how many 1/2 days (about 6+), but so far this year he's had 8 school days off ...... including when he had his appendix out, we're keeping our fingers crossed that he doesn't have too many more.

Holly had her first ever dancing solo last Saturday.  She said she forgot about cartwheels, but she did such an amazing job, I still can't believe that she did it and smiled at the age of 4!!!!!  She didn't want to take her medal off either.  After her performance she went to a friend from kindergarten's "Barbie" themed birthday party.  We then went out for dinner with my mum at the local pub to celebrate what Seth and Holly have achieved over the last 12 months.

Sunday we went as guests of the Dandenong Rangers Basketball Team & Dandenong Stadium to see Seth's friend DQ play.  They won by 4 points!!!  There was a very nice surprise when we got there.  We knew we were sitting in a corporate box but we didn't know it was catered too.  I also saw John and his family, one of the race car owners I met last year from the ride day I had at Phillip Island with

104

DQ that was organised via Challenge helping kids with cancer, it was good to catch up with him, even though he's not racing in the 944 Challenge Cup this year.

Seth will have his 4th last chemo via Lumbar Puncture next week. His blood test results from last week were exactly as we want to see them and his Oncology team are very happy with what his body is doing at the moment.

Next weekend is Stadium Stomp, Nikki and Team Stomping for Seth will stomp 7300+ stairs at the MCG all to raise money for the Leukaemia Foundation to aid research funding, which we feel is imperative as even since Seth was diagnosed in 2012, his prognosis has risen from 80+% to 85+% for a normal life expectancy.

If you're not smiling, why not, because Seth is,

Simon, Nikki, Seth and Holly


**16/07/15**

Hi,

Seth had his 4th last (Hopefully) chemo via I.V. last Thursday and we all made it through 5 days of steroids!

A little while ago I was asked if Seth would help promote Children's Cancer Institute at "Run Melbourne" to help raise money for them, which he is. That lead to them asking if he would also help with the media release of a new chemotherapy drug that specifically helps people with T-cell Acute Lymphoblastic Leukaemia or as it's known professionally - T A L L, exactly what Seth is fighting. As a family, we will do anything we can to help with awareness and so we gladly decided that we would help. Channel 2, 7 and 9 filmed us for the media release and I also did an interview over the phone for ABC's national radio and Seth was in the Sydney paper Sydney Morning Herald.

Friday, Seth and Holly enjoyed a day with thanks to Koala Kids at Horseback in Mornington. They spent the day learning about how to care for horses and how to ride them, this also lead to the Melbourne paper Herald Sun taking pics and Seth somehow managed to smile just the right way and he was in the paper earlier this week.

Saturday we loaded up the wagon and headed to Ballarat to stay with Seth and Holly's Poppy. On Sunday we were special guests of the North Ballarat Rebels TAC Cup football (Aussie rules for the overseas readers) club. It was their annual fundraiser for Ronald McDonald House Charities; they raised $3,500 which will go such a long way. Seth was given a 1 match contract that meant he had access all areas and also a player (Jake) to look after him. Although it rained and he couldn't go to the bench or on the ground at 1/4 and 3/4 time, he did go into the rooms and coaches box.

Monday night was time for Nikki to shine and she sure did shine! With a throat and chest infection she had our annual fundraiser for the Leukaemia Foundation. This year was at Village Cinema's Fountain Gate. She sold over 150 tickets, organised and drew the raffle, had 2 guys walk around in jeans (topless) rattling tins and the ladies certainly appreciated it because there were a lot of coins being dropped in the tins! A final figure has not been finalised yet as we are waiting for a few more donations that have been promised, but we are pleased with the amount that has been raised so far, the bank account is about $3,500 which will be deposited into the Leukaemia Foundation's bank next week.

Although everything happened at once, it has been months of planning and discussions with many different people. Every single second has been worth it! As for the title of this email, that is how I feel about what Nikki, Seth and Holly have achieved over the last few months that all fell into place this week.

The news links are:

Channel 2: https://www.youtube.com/watch?v=llKvlsiI1WU&feature=youtu.be

Channel 7: https://www.youtube.com/watch?v=91GmqOhAj7Q&feature=youtu.be

Channel 9: https://www.youtube.com/watch?v=WTfg1girYZ4&feature=youtu.be
ABC radio: https://soundcloud.com/childrens-cancer-inst/abcrn
Attached is the Herald Sun article, a behind the scenes pic of Seth and a bad pic of me giving a speech to the footy club about what Ronald McDonald House Charities have done for us. Phil, Jake and Seth are also pictured.
If you're not smiling, why not, because Seth is,
Seth, Holly, Nikki and Simon


**30/07/15**

Hi,
Since Seth's last blood test he has developed a cold of some sort, actually Holly has too and Nikki is into her sixth week. Over the weekend it was starting to look like he was getting an infection and a trip to hospital may be required. Luckily he didn't and we had a quiet weekend at home to recover. Unfortunately it meant that we cancelled Nikki's small birthday dinner, but the four of us had take away dinner at home, a birthday picnic of sorts on the floor in front of a movie.
In true Seth style, he was determined to go to school on Monday because he didn't want to miss sport. Unfortunately because the cold is still lingering, he didn't go to Kung Fu last night ...... he still did some training at home, he's determined to pass his Grade 2 grading in a month or so!
Holly went to dancing last Tuesday, she then spent the afternoon with her Nonna and although she has a cold, I was told she loved going shopping and getting new boots and also had something to say the whole time. Holly is definitely a chatterbox!
Seth will have another blood test next Wednesday and his third last I.V. on Thursday.
I am still waiting on donations for the Leukaemia Foundation that we have been promised. As soon as we receive them, I will let you know the exact total of all money being donated, it is over $3500.
If you're not smiling, why not, because Seth is,
Simon, Nikki, Seth & Holly




**6/08/15**

G'day,
After another blood test yesterday Seth went off to school and Holly went to Kinder. Not long after school started Nikki called me to say that a lot of kids in Grade 3 are off school sick with a few different illnesses, so to lessen the risk of infection and possible hospital admission I picked Seth up and worked from home.
Today we ventured down the freeway to the Children's Cancer Centre at Monash for his 3rd last I.V. chemo. During the consultation with his Oncologist, he was given the all clear for any physical signs of infection or virus and it should be ok for him to go back to school on Monday.
Seth now has 2 I.V. chemo's and 1 Lumbar Puncture left for his treatment of Acute Lymphoblastic Leukaemia! Early next month he will have his last Lumbar Puncture in the morning and 2nd last I.V. in the afternoon.
As we get closer to the end of treatment I can't help but think about what he's been through, what Holly has seen what Nikki and I have learnt and it reinforces my need to spread awareness, not only of ALL, but also the charities and foundations that have helped us. Then there's my desperate need to find a cure! That is why we look for ways to raise money, to provide experiences, to help with

awareness. Recently Nikki and "Team Stomping for Seth" stomped 7,300+ stairs at the MCG and held a movie night. With thanks to Pacific Magazines, Hilti Power Tools, My Chemist Fountain Gate, Ivy Lane Candle Works, Jeans West, Partyscape Event Planning, Amanda's Specialty Cakes and Desserts and as always, Seth's special friends Puffing Billy Tourist Railway we raised $3779.03 for the Leukaemia Foundation. The total also made the team the highest fundraisers for the second year in a row for L.F. at Stadium Stomp. Thanks to everyone!!!

If you're not smiling, why not, because Seth is,

Simon, Nikki, Seth & Holly


## 13/08/15

Hi all,

A very quick note this week.

I forgot to mention last week that we went to the footy with thanks to Challenge - Supporting Kids with Cancer.

Since last week we have had a reasonably quiet time together. At last!!! Seth has also suffered side effects from treatment; well he always does and never complains but this week he's had sore legs and headaches. It was a little bit of shock/scare for Nikki and I because he normally manages his pain and he hasn't had that amount of pain since when he was first being treated. He has a little bit of a cold, but is ok and is also back on the mend now that the monthly steroid dosage has been completed.

I wasn't going to send an update this week but it's been a little bit of a "milestone" week! He now has less than 2 months of chemo left (hopefully) and today is 3 years and 3 months (39 months) since Nikki and Seth took that scary first drive to Monash Medical Centre, Clayton.

If you're not smiling, why not, because Seth is,

Simon, Nikki, Seth and Holly.

P.S. A few have asked about my friends mum and her battle with Breast Cancer, she will have another operation tomorrow and hopefully she won't need anymore and can start her path to recovery.

P.P.S. A very close family friend lost her mum yesterday after a battle with illness R.I.P. Nikki and I are thinking of you and your girls and your grand children as you say goodbye to her.


## 20/08/15

Hi,

Seth has had a rough week, but he's still SMILING!

Last Friday night he and I went to the E.D. After about 4 hours in there, we came home. Monday he went to school. Monday night he developed a headache and a temp so we monitored him and after talking to the hospital E.D. he stayed home and we went into the Children's Cancer Centre on Tuesday for a check up. While there he had a blood test along with other tests and then some antibiotics and we headed home. Wednesday Nikki and I headed to work and Seth and Holly went to my mums. He developed a temperature in the late afternoon and the CCC and children's ward were full so off to the E.D. again. Nikki and I met them there. Seth and I left the E.D. about 10 or 10:30pm and enjoyed sleeping in our own beds. Today we headed back to the CCC for a check up, another blood test and more I.V. antibiotics. So far tests this week haven't developed any infections which means he's fighting a virus. The children's ward is still full so because of a few reasons, no high temperature, the Dr's knowing Nikki and I will go straight back to hospital and his blood levels rising being the main reasons, he is now home with me monitoring him until his temperature drops back and stays normal.  Hopefully we won't need to go back to the hospital until his next scheduled appointment in 2 weeks.

While all this is happening with Seth, Holly has also been unwell.  She has the same symptoms as Seth and she too won't stop smiling even though she isn't well.  She even missed dancing because of it and still practices at home instead of resting.

The picture attached of beads is Seth's "Beaded Journey".  Each bead signifies some sort of treatment since diagnosis 13/05/12, I.V. chemo, Lumbar Puncture, blood test, radiation treatment and the list goes on ....... The beads are now over 3 metres long that is a 1 metre ruler that they are around.

The other picture is Seth this afternoon showing off his Mickey Mouse bandaid (All bandaids are donated to the CCC).  It is because he's been hooked up with tubes since last night and is now "free" of them.  It's always a great relief when his port access is unhooked because he can be himself.

If you're not smiling, why not, because Seth is,

Simon, Nikki, Seth & Holly


## 2/09/15

Hi,

Today was Seth's last chemo via Lumber Puncture and second last chemo via I.V.  It was a long day! We left home at 9am and arrived home at 6:15pm.  Unfortunately over the last few weeks he's been knocked around a lot.  He had Mycoplasma (Pneumonia) which has run its course and gone after a 10 day course of strong antibiotics, but he is still fighting another viral bug.  Wednesday's blood test results came back low, but still high enough to go ahead with today.  While he was having his L.P. he also had a blood test and the results from today came back lower than yesterday.  It means that he is now neutropenic (low immunity to infection - 0.66) and can't go to school for the rest of the week.  It also means he needs another blood test Friday to see if he's still dropping.  Hopefully his 5 days of steroids that started tonight will help his body to lift by Friday and he'll return better results because if he keeps dropping as per yesterday and today's blood tests, he'll need to stop chemo for a week to let his body recover.  I was told that although it doesn't happen to everyone, kids often do what Seth's body is doing when they get close to the end of treatment.

He has about six weeks of chemo left!!!

Holly has a bug of some sort too, she won't let it beat her though, she just keeps going and going and going.... like an Energizer Bunny!

To all the dads, granddads and special people in kids lives - HAPPY FATHERS DAY for Sunday.

If you're not smiling, why not because Seth is

Simon, Nikki, Seth and Holly

P.S. Monday I lost a mate that I met at Parade College (high school) in 1989.  Ben Baird was always there, always listening, always asking how he could help.  We didn't see each other as much as we should, but we spoke on the phone regularly, infact I spoke to him 2 weeks ago and we were organising to catch up next week.  Ben died suddenly at home and would've celebrated his 41st birthday on the 24th of this month.  R.I.P. mate!


## 10/09/15

Hi all,

I hope everyone enjoyed Fathers Day, I certainly did and was spoilt with cuddles, watching DVD's and playing board games ...... of course presents too.

Seth has slowly been getting sick again since the last update.  His Neutrophil's dropped to 0.33 and also had a really bad headache among other symptoms on Tuesday night, so he and Nikki went to the E.D.  After the usual blood test and antibiotics being administered he also had Endone to help manage the pain.  The results returned that his blood levels were all low, so low he needed a blood transfusion; it actually ended up being 2 blood transfusions and being admitted to the ward.  He recovered very quickly after the transfusions and his smile returned.  He then had I.V. antibiotics every 6 hours and hourly monitoring by the nurses.... Nikki didn't sleep Tuesday night and I didn't last night.  Today he is home!!!  His Neutrophil's are 0.8 so still needs to be isolated from public areas and he needs to go to the CCC next Tuesday morning for another blood test and a check up.  The Dr's assured me it's because he's almost at the end of his treatment and his body is tired, no other reason.  It means no school until at least next Wednesday and the school term ends next Friday.  He has also started back on chemo tablets.

Seth has been having chemo for nearly 3 years and 4 months to date; he has one month left as long as all stays to plan.

Holly has enjoyed kinder, but missed dancing because Seth hasn't been well.  She's hoping to go back to dancing on Tuesday.  She's also not been terribly happy that the last 2 nights her big brother has not been home in his bed.

If you're not smiling, why not, because Seth is,

Simon, Nikki, Seth and Holly

P.S. Sorry for the pic being a little grainy, we were mucking around last night in hospital without the lights on with Seth's ipad.


## 17/09/15

Hi,

I have some great news... Seth went to school yesterday and today and he will enjoy "Footy colours day" tomorrow!  We went to the CCC on Tuesday for a checkup after his hospital admission last week and he is improving.  His white cells, red cells, platelets, Neutrophil's etc are steadily rising which is brilliant news, he's started back on oral chemo (don't tell anyone, but his mum & dad have started to sleep again).

Holly now has some sort of a bug, at first we thought it was a virus, possibly the one that sent Seth to hospital but she is having antibiotics and they are working.  She hasn't been herself for a few days and missed kinder and dancing this week but she is almost back to her normal self today.

Although Seth was in isolation we could see he was improving, so on Sunday so we snuck out of the house for a special meet and greet for Seth and Holly (Nikki too).  Seth was so excited because he'd been stuck inside the house for so long.  We went to the opening of a public park not far from here (in Lyndhurst) called "Livvi's Place" which is an all abilities playground.  The ambassador for the organisation that raises money to build the playgrounds is Jay Laga'aia (He's on Playschool, been on Star Wars and many, many Australian made TV series).  Jay has been very supportive for Seth, he's sent many messages to help Seth feel better when he's in hospital, and he even sang Seth a song to help him sleep when I told Jay that Seth was having trouble sleeping.  Jay was working in New Zealand when he started sending messages; it just shows how small the world is.  We watched Jay perform and then we had a chat while he was packing up and loading the car to head back to the airport (he lives in Sydney).  Although Holly didn't want to have  pic taken with Jay, both she and Seth were full of smiles after we left and we all hope to see him again soon.  Jay even wrote "It was lovely to see my mate Seth and his sister Holly and their mum and dad. He's a real life superhero!" on his Twitter page which made us all feel very special and very grateful for Jay to chat even though he was so busy and so short on time.  As a dad it was also touching to see Seth so happy with Jay, so much so that Seth gave Jay the gentle giant a hug goodbye, Seth NEVER does that to people he has just met.

109

Not long now until Seth has his last chemo via I.V.  I was chatting to one of the specialist nurses at the CCC while we were there about how excited we are and how Seth seems to be a little more happy with himself as we get closer to what will hopefully be the end of his treatment and she said that she and the staff are too.  Like all of you, they have watched Seth's journey, they've watched Holly grow and also watched Nikki and I learn.  She said they look forward to the end of treatment for their patients too.  It is a reminder to me that the hospital staff are humble humans too, I'm sure I've forgotten at times.

Have a great week!

If you're not smiling, why not, because Seth is,

Seth, Holly, Nikki & Simon

## 1/10/15

G'day,

Today Seth had his last blood test for chemo!  He will have blood tests still, but today was for his chemo dosage.

Better still... Seth had his last I.V. chemo this afternoon!  He has 5 days of steroids and 10 days of chemo tablets left, then that's it... FINISHED.  So far we are 3 years, 4 & 1/2 months since he went to the E.D.  We still need to be careful with illnesses like Chicken Pox etc. and he'll also have antibiotics twice a day, 3 times a week until mid January.

Since my last update we went to the races at Caulfield Race Course with Camp Quality.  We all had so much fun playing Jumbo Jenga, coits and croquet as well as checking out jumping castles and watching the horses run past.  We even caught up with a few people from the Leukaemia Foundation!

110

Seth still has a slightly runny nose, but has almost fully recovered from Pneumonia and is looking forward to going back to school next week.... he hasn't been for 5 or 6 weeks.

If you're not smiling, why not, because Seth is,

Seth, Holly, Nikki & Simon

P.S. In the pic is Liz from the CCC helping Seth with his last few beads and his "Last chemo" bead for his beaded journey.  They had footy colours day so Holly wore her jumper as a dress!  There is also a smash cake that is donated by Naughty Nush Smash Cakes to all the kids when they end treatment. It is made from chocolate and has over 1/2 a kilogram of mixed lollies inside.  It is literally a smash cake that is how you open it, with a rubber mallet!

**6/10/15**

I can hardly hold it in!!!!!!

Hi all,

This is a very quick note to say that this morning, before school Seth had his last steroid tablet! He's very close to finishing chemo, infact if you don't know; he'll have his last chemo tablet this Saturday, 10/10 a real 10 out of 10 day!

I was trying to wait for Saturday, but he has achieved so much, I had to share this pic and news with you!

If you're not smiling, why not, because Seth is,

Simon, Nikki, Seth and Holly :)

**11/10/15**

Hi all,

This update has a few newbie's, I send out updates about Seth and us and this one is definitely one of the hardest ones for me to write!

It is hard because Nikki and I are so overwhelmed with amazing emotion, we don't know how to explain it.

Yesterday we woke and Seth took his LAST chemotherapy tablet!!!!

Yesterday the 10th of October 2015 was day 1,246 - 3 years, 5 months and 28 days since we went to the G.P. and subsequently at approximately 7pm, Nikki and Seth went to Monash E.D. in Clayton (13/05/12 - Mothers Day) and Seth came home after staying in hospital for 13 days with a diagnosis of T-Cell, Acute Lymphoblastic Leukaemia and had already had a few operations, blood transfusions, blood tests and lots of other stuff.

Since that day, Seth has endured and smiled through nearly all of it -

20 lumbar punctures, 8 days of radiation, 70 rounds of chemotherapy (some rounds lasting 10 days), 2 bone marrow aspirations, 16 tests on his heart, kidney, bladder & chest, 4 inter muscular injections, 13 miscellaneous tests, 20 blood transfusions, 10 platelet transfusions, 3 plasma transfusions, 1 artificial plasma transfusion, 216 blood tests & port accesses, 81 visits to the children's cancer centre, 10 admissions to the ward (with stays up to 13 days), 14 ED admissions, 43 finger pricks, 2 surgeries, 10 physiotherapist sessions, 6 months of Occupational Therapy & Oral chemo every day for the last 2 and a half years and steroids. Seth has stopped his chemotherapy and hopefully after a couple of monthly checkups with the Oncologist he will be able to have his port removed & then in about 6 months he will be reimmunised once his immunity starts to pick back up.

Seth and Holly wrote a list of friends they wanted to celebrate by having a BBQ with. It truly was a day to remember, a friend of Seth (and us), A.J. owns Yummo Ice Cream in Mornington and also an ice cream van, he brought the van over for everyone to have a soft serve or Gelati, A.J. donated to Seth and Seth thought long and hard and decided to ask that if anyone wanted to donate for their ice cream, he would give it to Camp Quality... Seth is going to give $136.50 to CQ on behalf of A.J.

We also had a few Corvettes come over to give the kids a ride. We can't thank the guys and girls from Corvettes of Melbourne enough!!! They took everyone that wanted to go for a ride and they were here for about3 hours! Michael thanks so much for organising the cars (Congrats to Joel on his first trip in Dads Vette), you all have massive hearts of gold and I hope you didn't get too dizzy driving around. OH!!!! I also had the pleasure of driving the 2011 Corvette Grand Sport, thanks Tania and Graham; it was an experience I will remember.

While all of that was happening, thanks to Dave, Amanda, Tara, Candice, Katrina and Belinda for helping Nikki organise the food.

I took lots of pics and Holly kept hiding from me, I snapped a few of her, but not many! That got me thinking about what pic I'd attach to this email and I decided that the pic of Seth taking his last tablet at approximately 8 a.m. was the one. Then I thought there's one more, Nikki does what needs to be done and works bloody hard with no complaint and rarely makes an appearance in a pic, so I found a pic with her from yesterday that says it all, that explains yesterday perfectly, a picture that says a thousand words (Tania the car's owner is driving)!!!

This morning we woke and Seth had day 1 post chemo and not 1 tablet required, not even an antibiotic (That's tomorrow). He will still have blood tests and monthly visits to the Children's Cancer Centre for at least one year. They will slowly become less and after about five years they will be twice a year and eventually he will have annual visits until October 2025, he'll drive us on his "P Plates" to his last and finally post Leukaemia check up.

We now wait and see what his blood results come back with when he has his next test at the end of

112

this month, it is a very slim possibility that he'll have day surgery to have his access port removed before Christmas but when his body is ok, that is when it will happen.

If you're not smiling, why not, because Seth is,

Simon, Nikki, Seth & Holly

**29/10/15**

Hi,

We've been busy enjoying the first month post chemo! We went on a camp with Camp Quality the weekend after his last chemo and it was so much fun. We went to the city and investigated the city, National Gallery of Victoria and then Hosier Lane which is one of three lanes in Melbourne where it is legal to create art by way of graffiti.

Seth has also had his first post chemo blood test and check up with his Oncology Dr today. All is great, his body is doing exactly what they want it to do... today the contact was made with the surgical department to have his access port removed, that's how great his results are, so it looks like he'll have another op before Christmas to have it removed.

Last Friday the world lost a wonderful woman, Ronnie, she is the owner of my work's wife. Mike and Ronnie have helped Nikki and I throughout Seth's illness and Ronnie made sure he was ok and Nikki, Holly and I were coping. Today was her funeral and she would've loved it! R.I.P. Ronnie.

Also, a work colleague's daughter is in the ICU at Monash. Ayla turned 12 on Monday and had an operation that was expected to have both legs amputated below her knees. She returned from her op with both hands and feet attached, there was enough viable tissue found and she will hopefully be up and walking again soon. She was diagnosed with Necrotising Myosotis. As you know, Seth loves Collingwood Football Club in the AFL and they sent her a few posters and a card signed by a few players because she loves them too. After Seth's check up today, we had a coffee with her Dad and it was great to see him smiling and telling me about how great everyone has been to help Ayla get better. Her Mum and Dad are living at Ronald McDonald House so they can be with her, as you know, we use the RMH Family Room and now we know someone using the house, thank you all who donates.

If you're not smiling, why not, because Seth is,

Simon, Nikki, Seth and Holly

**26/11/15**

Hi everyone,

What a month of success!

Firstly, my last update I mentioned Ayla turning 12 in the ICU and fighting a terrible flesh eating infection called Necrotizing Myosotis. Seth, Holly and I met her this afternoon and I am extremely pleased to say that she is now on the ward, cruising in a wheel chair for more time than her O.T. wants as a minimum amount and all surgery has now been completed. Ayla has survived the infection, still has all her limbs and will hopefully be home for Christmas!!! When talking to her dad Paul that works at one of the branches of my work... I don't know how to describe the smile on his face or his wife and Ayla's mum Rachel. It was relief, happiness, fear for the future, and a lot more relief and happiness rolled into one smile.

Last weekend we went to Santa's Magical Kingdom for Camp Quality's Christmas Party. It was great to see Margaret from Silvers Circus again. We loved the whole afternoon and catching up with the familiar faces of staff and Volunteers. When I asked Seth and Holly what the best part was, they said the Circus and then decorating and eating a ginger bread man.

Unfortunately late last week a very good friend and also Seth and my Barber, Andrew lost his mum. I had the pleasure of meeting Janet and she definitely will be missed, not only by her 6 kids, 12 grand kids and 1 great grand kid, but everyone that was ever fortunate to meet her.

Today Seth had another blood test and this afternoon was his monthly post chemo check up. All results are where they need to be and his Neutrophil's (immunity) is 7.7, that's exactly where an 8 year old boy should be! I checked with regard to his access port removal and was told that it should happen in the next 2 weeks. If it does, this Christmas will be the first Christmas since diagnosis 13/05/12 without it in his body, infact it will be the first Christmas post chemotherapy!!!!!

Holly has had all her prep orientations for school too. She is more than ready to start school next year... I'm not sure if I'm ready for her to start school!!! This Saturday is her dancing concert and she is very excited! It's not her first concert, but it is her first concert with this dance school and she has been practicing up and down the hallway all week.

Nikki has resigned from her current temporary job and will finish Friday. She went to a job interview Wednesday last week, got offered the job 10ish Thursday morning and received the employment contract by about 1pm Thursday. It's a relief to know Nikki now has job security and will start on Monday.

Mrs R, don't worry, I've been busy enjoying all of the above... I have had an amazing offer to go for a cruise in a few Supercars in a few weeks, it's a second once in a lifetime experience that was offered from Jim that gave me my first once in a lifetime experience. I'm not giving anything at all away because someone that reads this email is coming and I'd rather show pics to you all after we do it but the Lamborghini Gallardo Seth and I had December last year is one of the two cars we'll be passengers in.

If you're not smiling, why not, because Seth is,

Simon, Nikki, Seth and Holly


**10/12/15**

Hi everyone,

Christmas is coming fast for us this year! This time last year as I write, Seth was admitted to hospital and ultimately wasn't too well on Christmas Day, but we did have Christmas at home.

I am writing a quick update because we have had some amazing things happen and I had a dream come true last weekend.

Firstly, we were at the Challenge - Supporting kids with cancer Christmas Party a few weeks ago and I got to go for a ride in a Delorean, it was definitely a great experience. Seth and Holly had heaps of fun on the rides and seeing some friends they've met throughout Seth's treatment. I also caught up with an ex Paradian that I went to school with.

Holly had her end of year dance concert and she has improved so much since changing schools! We went to her end of year kinder celebration last night. It was a great picnic and even better to watch her and her kinder friends sing some songs. Next Wednesday, Seth and Holly finish for the year!

Nikki has started a new job and is loving it. She's back in a corporate environment and loves that she is setting payroll and AP back up for the company and starting company procedures to get the department back on the right track.

My dream that came true;

I organised with Jim whom owns the Lamborghini Gallardo I borrowed last year to cruise around our housing estate with Seth showing his mates the real life "Hot Wheels" car, to have an hour of cruising to help bring back Aidan's smile. Aidan is Ayla's older brother. Ayla is improving every day and will hopefully learn to walk again in the not too distant future. We met up with Jim and a mate of his, Steve. Jim organised for his Lambo and Ferrari Testarossa to be there to cruise around. Then Jim opened a roller door, drove an AC Cobra Replica out and offered me a drive!!! The hour turned into 2 or 2 & 1/2 hours and it is arguable as to who had the biggest smile (kids or dads), we all became big kids driving the cars. I have always liked the AC Cobra's and hoped one day I'd be a passenger, never did I dream I'd get to drive one AND to have Seth in the passenger seat, WOW!!! Thanks Jim.

From us, to you, we hope you have a great Christmas!!

If you're not smiling, why not, because Seth is,

Simon, Nikki, Seth & Holly


## 16/12/15

Hi everyone,

I thought my last update was it until after Christmas but I have to tell you that this morning Seth had his access port removed and we are now recovering at home! After weeks of waiting and to be told yesterday morning that it won't happen until at least late January, Nikki found a Paediatric Surgeon that has such a massive heart, he gave us possibly one of the best Christmas presents ever by adding Seth to his operating list for this morning. By 1pm yesterday, the surgeon was confirmed, the anaesthetist was confirmed and the hospital had sent the paperwork to be filled out. He didn't have the operation at Monash, but he is very happy that his port is out and even happier that there are no stitches, but glue instead! This pic was taken an hour after he woke from his operation.

If you're not smiling, why not, because Seth is,

Simon, Nikki, Seth & Holly

P.S. He will have his last antibiotic tablet on Friday night so will spend Christmas with the memory of Leukaemia, not 1 tablet, not anything inside his body, just a 8 year old boy named Seth!

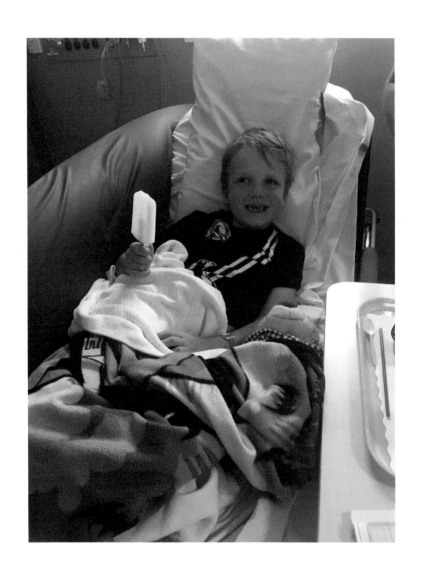

# 2016

**28/01/16**

Hi Everyone,
It's been a little over 3 months since Seth had his last chemo tablet.
We hope that everyone enjoyed Christmas and had a great New Year!
We went to Sydney for a few days before Christmas and enjoyed stopping at the Dog on the Tucker Box and Big Merino along with going to the Aquarium at Darling Harbour. Seth and Holly got spoilt rotten from Santa and of course their grandparents. We also went to Ballarat and visited the Wildlife Park there.
School for us is back on Monday. It's a big day because not only does Seth start Grade 4, but Holly has her first day of school and starts Prep. It's hard to imagine that when Seth was diagnosed, Holly was 13 months old and now she's about to be a school kid! It also means those swimming lessons (which Seth couldn't do whilst on treatment due to his low immunity), Seth's Kung Fu and Holly's dancing all start for the year.
The pic attached is Seth's "Beaded Journey". It is donated by CCCF for all children to do that are receiving treatment in the CCC. Each bead signifies a blood test, x-ray, I.V. chemo, radiation etc. Here's the bit I (Simon) can't "get my head around" and I was part of the treatment journey for Seth, it is just a little over 3.6 metres long!!!!!
I am on leave from work and loving being a home Dad. I am still working from home on a casual basis, but loving getting all the jobs I haven't had time to do done like pulling out Yukka's, taking out a garden bed to make the kids play area bigger and I am even planning on painting the inside of the house once school is sorted and both Seth and Holly are settled.
Nikki is enjoying her new job. There have been some changes in staff, but she's enjoying the challenges that get thrown at her.
If you're not smiling, why not, because Seth is,
Simon, Nikki, Seth & Holly

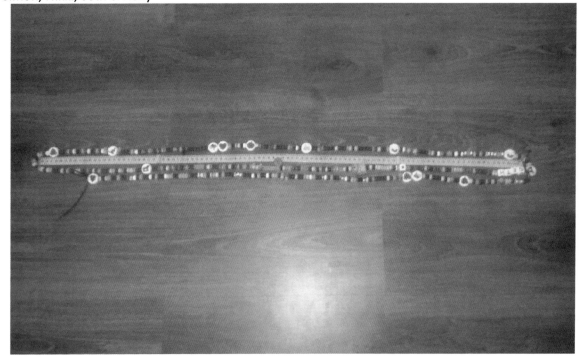

**1/03/16**

Hi all,

Since my last update, school has started, Holly's dancing has started and both Seth and Holly have started swimming lessons. I'm still on leave, but working a few hours every few days to keep me lubricated. I'm also painting the inside if the house ... every room and a complete colour change to the walls and architraves! It is frustrating at times, but at the end of each day I can step back, look at my achievement and be satisfied that I did it. My Dad helped me on the first day to get the job rolling and show me the correct way to use a roller, he has saved me a lot of time and stress.

Seth's immunity is now consistent and high enough to visit an indoor public pool!!! We even had the pleasure of sitting in the waiting room at a doctors surgery recently and although it is possibly one of the worst ways to spend time, I cherished every minute with Seth sitting next to me because he hasn't been to the general doctor's surgery since his blood test on Mother's Day 2012 which subsequently resulted in him going to Hospital and coming home 13 days later fighting Leukaemia (I think we may have been recently, again with Holly, but it is something to have him there).

Holly has been to her ENT specialist and also another specialist to have a hearing test. We will see her ENT in a few weeks to get the results but I was told 1 grommet is still in 1 ear and is blocking her hearing due to it being dislodged. Hopefully that doesn't mean an operation, but I and Nikki suspect she will need one.

Seth had another check up at the CCC (Children's Cancer Centre) and all is still looking good and his blood is doing all things it should be. He may start re immunising next month!

Seth had his 9th birthday too!!! February 14th. We and some mates of his ventured down to Dingley Village Adventure Golf to celebrate his first post chemotherapy birthday. We all had so much fun! DVAG set up the room with an Avengers theme and Captain America (Seth's fave) paid a visit. I think Captain America loved Seth's smile because he took the kids all out for a full course of mini golf and then gave out lolly bags while his wife (SSHHHH the kids don't know he wasn't the real deal) took heaps of photo's for us. The staff at DVAG, especially Gabby, Rob and Caitlin were amazing and we cannot thank them enough!

Last weekend we ventured to Cottlesbridge to celebrate a cousins wedding. Nikki's little pocket rocket took the bride to her ceremony and Nikki was one of the bridesmaids ... I hope she signed her name correctly as a witness on the paperwork! Seth was one of the ring bearers too; it was so good to see him take on the responsibility. I took heaps of pics and Holly simply made new friends, taught and learnt games and was always smiling. So yes, there is now another "Mrs Sleep" and I don't think she could be any happier after watching her through the camera lense. CONGRATS Damian and Sandra. Seth also pointed out that her initials are now the same as his and mine, Seth was happy about that.

If you're not smiling, why not, because Seth is,

Simon, Nikki, Seth and Holly

P.S. In my last update I didn't mention our visit to Puffing Billy. It was a cold and wet day but we made the most of it and had so much fun. I met Kate, Lily and Harrison. I've known Kate via Facebook for about 2 years and we finally met face to face. Lily and Harrison are 2 of her kids. Harrison is an extremely cheeky and loving boy and I am trying to work out how to raise money (Which is why I didn't mention it in my last update, but can't find a way) for Kate, his mum to buy a portable crane to aid in getting him in and out of the bath.

This is taken from his Facebook page;

Harrison is a very special little boy, who was born with a genetic syndrome called, Velocardiofacial syndrome (22q11 syndrome, DiGeorge syndrome).

It affects approx 1 in 2000-3000 persons and is the most common genetic syndrome associated with cleft palates and the second most common genetic syndrome associated with congenital heart defects.

99% of the VCFS population will have a learning difficulty

30% will develop a mental illness

Harrison was diagnosed as having one of the worst cases of VCFS his genetic doctor had seen, because Harrison also has a developmental brain malformation called polymicrogyria (PMG), which means literally many small folds of the brain.PMG is not a common occurrence in the VCFS population but it has been noted. Harrison is also micro cephalic, which means his head size is more than 2 standard sizes smaller than the average person of the same age and sex.

Harrison also suffers from epilepsy; he has cerebral palsy, asthma and suffered from devastating reflux, which he has had surgery to manage. He is unable to walk, talk, and is fed through a feeding tube (PEG) directly into his stomach. He is also the most amazing, happy and beautiful soul I have had the pleasure of loving!!

The crane is approximately $6,000, if not more. If you have any ideas or contacts please let me know and I will pass your info to Kate or contact via his Facebook page to his mum directly: https://www.facebook.com/Helping-Harrison-296596037091813/info/?tab=page_info

## 29/04/16

Hi,

I am back at work! It was a brilliant break and now we're getting used to school, work, home balance.

Since my last update Seth & I flew to Adelaide and spent the day at the Electrolux oven making factory. It was an early rise at 4:30am and home after 8pm but we both enjoyed the robotics etc. The same day Holly had an operation to take the grommet out that hadn't fallen out of her ear yet. Yesterday was a follow up appointment with her specialist and it is healing well. A little while ago she also had a hearing test and we were told she is slightly deaf in one ear. After her appointment yesterday her specialist said that both ears are growing correctly and she has a high chance of having normal hearing soon because her body is mending her ear.

Holly also had her 5th birthday and she decided to have a Devonshire Tea party at The Old Cheese Factory in Berwick. Everyone, parents and kids loved it! It was so much fun and all her friends also dressed up as princesses that was the final perfect touch.

Holly is really enjoying her dancing classes and Seth is still having a break from Kung Fu. He needs to do something, so he has swimming lessons and plays basketball, he's also hoping to start piano lessons this weekend to compliment his guitar. Both Seth and Holly are grabbing life with both hands and making the most of it.

Seth has passed 6 months since his last chemo tablet and also had his 6 month post chemo check up. All is as expected and he's had all his immunisations. His next blood test will also check that the immunisations have "taken" so he won't need anymore. He's still having monthly check ups and his growth spurt that started when chemo stopped seems to have slowed but he is still taller than some of his mates so the chemo side effect of slowing his growth has definitely gone.

It's apple picking season! We've been to a localish farm a few times to stock up on apples straight off the trees. We all love going there and picking our own.

Seth and Holly have also had their school athletics carnival and they both came home with smiles and ribbons. Holly loved participating more than watching as she has done in the last few years.

If you're not smiling, why not, because Seth is,

Simon, Nikki, Seth & Holly

P.S. A friend is fighting hard against a cancer relapse (for several months). Although he is in his 60's it doesn't discriminate and he's been giving it a good fight. Hopefully he'll be able to leave palliative care and go home soon, he keeps talking about going back to work too. Please keep him, his wife, kids, grand kids etc in your thoughts.

## 13/05/16

Hi all,

May 13, 2012 was Mothers Day and was also the day Seth had a blood test before lunch. Approximately 6pm the phone rang, it was the G.P. calling and by about 7pm Seth and Nikki were on their way to the E.D. at Monash Hospital. That was four years ago today, four years ago our lives and many around us changed. He is also now just over seven months since his last chemo tablet and other than having a cold, he's as his Dr said "a normal 9 year old boy". Next week he'll have his monthly blood test that will check his blood including the immunisations he had last month. All going well and he won't need another immunisation because they have all worked.

Over the days leading up to today I have thought about the last four years. The people we've met, the opportunities we've had, the people we've lost and all the people that have helped us. There is so many that have helped us from food in the early days of diagnosis to phone calls to see how we are to experiences and the list goes on and on. I was also in deep thought about what he's lost, what was taken from him, some of his early school days and childhood but he has been a champion all the way. He's had over 200 needles, I think it's more than 10 blood transfusions to keep him alive, not to mention the radiation and of course chemo along with everything else.

I remember about 7:30pm trying to "hold it together" to call my boss to tell him something is wrong with Seth and I won't be in tomorrow (Monday). From that call all the way to right now he and his family have been there for us, all four of us. Their help, support, compassion and understanding will stay in our hearts forever. For that on behalf of my family I thank you from the bottom of my heart, I really do not know how I and Nikki would've got to today without your help Mike, Damian and Renee.

There is also Ben (R.I.P.) that from the first call was always there, he just had a knack of knowing he was needed and was just simply "there". Alan, Seth's Godfather is the other, he and his family, like Ben were just there. I know there are others; you know who you are and thank you.

Today Seth went to school but I picked him up before lunch because his cold has taken his energy and now after a few hours on the couch he's feeling better although the tissues aren't too far from reach.

Seth was 5, Holly was just over 1 when Seth got sick and to see them grow and see how they live life now is amazing. Sure they fight, but their bond is so strong, so amazing to watch how they look after and look out for each other is amazing. Holly has grown into an amazingly strong girl and still makes sure she has some things for herself like dancing, but her brother is rarely from her thoughts when they're not together.

If you're not smiling, why not, because Seth is,

Simon, Nikki, Seth & Holly

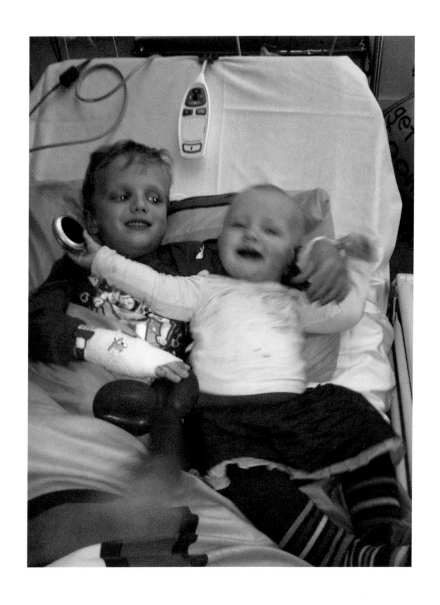

**10/10/16**

Hi all

Today is 1 year since Seth had his last chemotherapy tablet!

He's had monthly check ups at the Children's Cancer Centre and all is so far so good, now he will have checkups every 2 months. He had his first year check up last Friday and as far as his body is concerned, he's a normal 9 year old boy. His original Oncology Doctor has been on leave since about 6 months after his diagnosis and recently returned to work. Seth remembered her and was very pleased that he got to see her. She couldn't believe how much he'd grown. I showed her pics of Holly and again, she couldn't believe how much Holly has grown into a beautiful girl.

Seth has had a few things happen recently, his bike was stolen from our garage and was then given a replacement from Corvette's of Melbourne car club, he joined a basketball team and played U12's D Grade and the team made it to the Semi Final, he joined Hoop Time (Basketball) at school and his team have progressed to the next stage, he's had a few sleepovers and slept over at a few friends (this is very wonderful, he wouldn't do it until recently), he's continuing with guitar lessons and started piano lessons (he's writing his own music too), he even went on a school camp and lots more stuff he couldn't do until his treatment stopped.

Both Seth and Holly have started swimming lesson too!

Holly is still madly dancing and looking forward to the end of year concert. She also joined Dance Club at school and will be on stage at her school Carnival on October 23. She's already telling me that she's ready for Grade 1 next year!

As you can see from the pic, Holly has always been by her big brothers side. From lying on his bed in hospital when he was first admitted to when Seth was at his highest weight gain and hair loss to last night before going to bed. They've grown so much and are best friends.

If you're not smiling, why not, because Seth is,

Simon, Nikki, Seth and Holly

*Now Seth has finished treatment for one year he has blood tests and checkups at the hospital every two months.  As he progresses further away from diagnosis and end of treatment, the less frequent his blood tests and checkups will be.  They will slowly lessen to eventually be an annual check up until he is ten years post chemotherapy.  That appointment will not only be a big closing of a huge chapter in our lives but he will also be 18 and will drive his mum, dad and sister to the appointment.*
*If you're not smiling, why not, because Seth is.*

# Our family's life fighting Leukaemia

This journal is a collation of emails I sent to friends, families and supporters through our fight against Leukaemia, Acute Lymphoblastic T-Cell. Seth was 5, just started school earlier in the year and healthy. May 13, 2012 was Mothers Day in Australia and he had an enlarged stomach and what we thought was a rash. As a family my wife Nikki, daughter Holly (13 months old), myself and Seth went to our Doctor and we were told that the rash was bruising. A blood test was done and we were told to stay home in isolation until the next morning when the results were due back. As you read you'll discover what happened later that Sunday night and continue with us until one year after his last chemotherapy tablet. Seth had Chemotherapy, Radiation, Steroids and the list goes on from 13/05/12 to 10/10/14... Three and a half years.

Printed in Great Britain
by Amazon